I0100243

Declassified in Part - Sanitized Copy Approved for Release 2016/07/19 : CIA-RDP79T00936A009100010001-5

The President's Daily Brief

1 January 1971

47

50X1

Declassified in Part - Sanitized Copy Approved for Release 2016/07/19 : CIA-RDP79T00936A009100010001-5

Declassified in Part - Sanitized Copy Approved for Release 2016/07/19 : CIA-RDP79T00936A009100010001-5

THE PRESIDENT'S DAILY BRIEF

1 January 1971

PRINCIPAL DEVELOPMENTS

Enemy military activity has increased in Cambodia's northwest provinces. *(Page 1)*

_____ 50X1 50X1
_____ *(Page 2)*   50X1

Elements of a North Vietnamese Army Division appear to be preparing to return to northern Laos. *(Page 3)*

Sino-Soviet relations have slumped a bit. *(Page 5)*

Declassified in Part - Sanitized Copy Approved for Release 2016/07/19 : CIA-RDP79T00936A009100010001-5

Declassified in Part - Sanitized Copy Approved for Release 2016/07/19 : CIA-RDP79T00936A009100010001-5

CAMBODIA: Current Situation

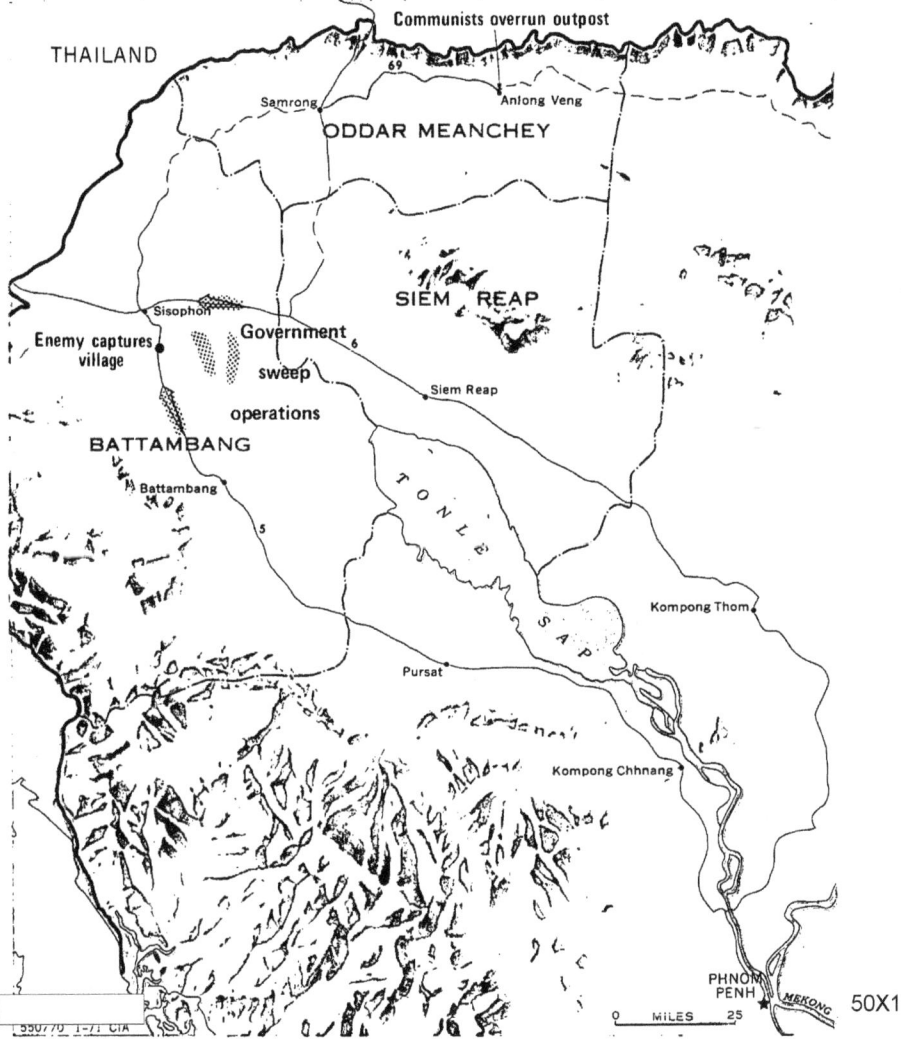

THAILAND

Communists overrun outpost

Samrong

Anlong Veng

ODDAR MEANCHEY

Sisophon

SIEM REAP

Enemy captures
village

Government

sweep

Siem Reap

operations

BATTAMBANG

Battambang

T O N L É   S A P

Kompong Thom

Pursat

Kompong Chhnang

PHNOM
PENH

MEKONG

0   MILES   25

50X1

Declassified in Part - Sanitized Copy Approved for Release 2016/07/19 : CIA-RDP79T00936A009100010001-5

Declassified in Part - Sanitized Copy Approved for Release 2016/07/19 : CIA-RDP79T00936A009100010001-5

CAMBODIA

Enemy forces recently captured a village and a bridge on Route 5 in Battambang Province, less than ten miles south of the crossroads town of Sisophon.

> *This marks the first time the Communists have cut the western land access to Battambang city, the country's second largest urban center. The Communist advance was carried out in the face of a government operation _____ to clear the area around Sisophon.*

50X1

Farther north, Communist forces have moved to within 15 miles of Samrong, the poorly defended capital of remote Oddar Meanchey Province. The enemy push toward Samrong began with the overrunning of a small Cambodian garrison at Anlong Veng on Route 69 on 21 December. Since then, the Communists have captured several other lightly defended government positions as they moved west along the road. Other enemy troops are threatening the government's few remaining outposts north of Samrong, near the Thai border.

50X1

> *The increase in Communist activity in Oddar Meanchey may be intended in part to distract government forces trying to clear roads farther south toward Siem Reap Province. Oddar Meanchey is impoverished in both population and resources, and its loss would not be a major setback to the government; Phnom Penh in fact has already written it off.*

1

Declassified in Part - Sanitized Copy Approved for Release 2016/07/19 : CIA-RDP79T00936A009100010001-5

FOR THE PRESIDENT ONLY

JORDAN-FEDAYEEN

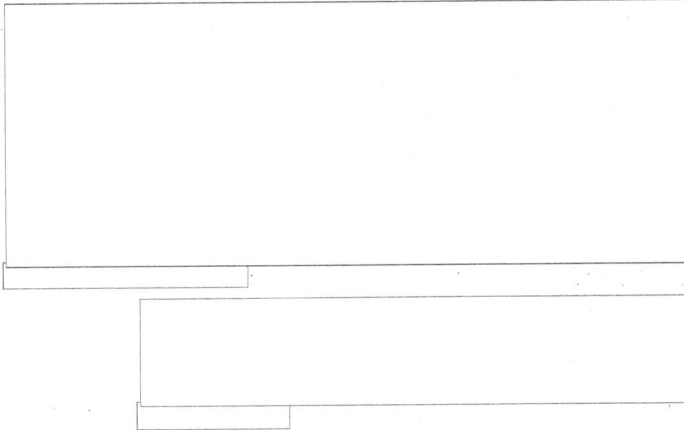

50X1

50X1

50X1

50X1

2

Declassified in Part - Sanitized Copy Approved for Release 2016/07/19 : CIA-RDP79T00936A009100010001-5

NVA 312th Division May Return To Laos

CHINA

BURMA

CHINA

NORTH

Hanoi

VIETNAM

Ban Ban

MEKONG

Plaine des Jarres

Long Tieng

GULF

Cho Si

OF

312th Division relocating

TONKIN

Vinh

THAILAND

Vientiane

18—

DEMARCATION LINE

SOUTH

VIETNAM

THAILAND

0   100
MILES

CAMBODIA

550771 1-71 CIA

50X1

Declassified in Part - Sanitized Copy Approved for Release 2016/07/19 : CIA-RDP79T00936A009100010001-5

Declassified in Part - Sanitized Copy Approved for Release 2016/07/19 : CIA-RDP79T00936A009100010001-5

LAOS - NORTH VIETNAM

There are indications in intercepts that elements of the North Vietnamese Army 312th Division--which has been located near Vinh since withdrawing from Laos last summer--may be on the move. Rear service groups at Vinh, for example, have reported that some 3,000 troops would be moving through the Cho Si railroad complex in early January.

The pattern of these movements suggest the 312th is returning to Laos. Cho Si is a major transshipment point for personnel and supplies headed for northern Laos. Troops returning to the Hanoi area from Vinh could also be routed through Cho Si, but this seems less likely.

The 312th was introduced into Laos for the first time last year following the government's capture of the Plaine des Jarres. It was used principally as a rear guard security force. The main burden of the effort to clear the Plaine and push toward the government's Long Tieng complex belonged to the NVA 316th Division. The 312th's return could be part of a buildup for intensified dry season action or a specific response to the government's harassment operation at Ban Ban.

3

Declassified in Part - Sanitized Copy Approved for Release 2016/07/19 : CIA-RDP79T00936A009100010001-5

Declassified in Part - Sanitized Copy Approved for Release 2016/07/19 : CIA-RDP79T00936A009100010001-5

USSR

50X1

4

Declassified in Part - Sanitized Copy Approved for Release 2016/07/19 : CIA-RDP79T00936A009100010001-5

Declassified in Part - Sanitized Copy Approved for Release 2016/07/19 : CIA-RDP79T00936A009100010001-5

NOTES

USSR-China: Yesterday a <u>Pravda</u> editorial rebuked the Chinese for Peking's attack last week on "Soviet revisionist imperialism" in Eastern Europe. Both states have now broken their suspension of full dress polemics. These outbursts together with the collapse of the Sino-Soviet river navigation talks on 19 December have somewhat negated the tenuous signs of improvement in state-to-state relations.

50X1

Poland: Poland's new chief of state, Jozef Cyrankiewicz, and Foreign Minister Jedrychowski emphatically expressed hope for improvement in US-Polish relations in private conversations with Ambassador Stoessel at a year-end diplomatic reception in Warsaw. Cyrankiewicz showed a special interest in economic ties, and Jedrychowski confirmed our evaluation that there would be no change in Polish foreign policy under the new leadership. Jedrychowski added that Warsaw's policy of detente would, if anything, be intensified. Under this rubric, he told the Ambassador he wants to talk further about improving bilateral relations.

5

Declassified in Part - Sanitized Copy Approved for Release 2016/07/19 : CIA-RDP79T00936A009100010001-5

Declassified in Part - Sanitized Copy Approved for Release 2016/07/19 : CIA-RDP79T00936A009100010001-5

Top Secret

Declassified in Part - Sanitized Copy Approved for Release 2016/07/19 : CIA-RDP79T00936A009100010001-5

Declassified in Part - Sanitized Copy Approved for Release 2016/07/19 : CIA-RDP79T00936A009100020001-4

The President's Daily Brief

2 January 1971

50

Top Secret

50X1

Declassified in Part - Sanitized Copy Approved for Release 2016/07/19 : CIA-RDP79T00936A009100020001-4

Declassified in Part - Sanitized Copy Approved for Release 2016/07/19 : CIA-RDP79T00936A009100020001-4

THE PRESIDENT'S DAILY BRIEF

2 January 1971

PRINCIPAL DEVELOPMENTS

Peking's New Year pronouncement is cautious in its claims of progress. *(Page 1)*

50X1

(Page 2)

50X1

Venezuela is making tentative moves toward bringing Cuba into the inter-American system. *(Page 3)*

Declassified in Part - Sanitized Copy Approved for Release 2016/07/19 : CIA-RDP79T00936A009100020001-4

Declassified in Part - Sanitized Copy Approved for Release 2016/07/19 : CIA-RDP79T00936A009100020001-4

COMMUNIST CHINA

Peking's New Year pronouncement, appearing as a joint People's Daily - Red Flag - Liberation Army Journal *editorial on 31 December, is remarkably cautious in its claims of progress. For example, although party building at higher administrative echelons has been the first order of domestic business for the past year and a half, the editorial contains little self-congratulation over the pace of the program and fails even to cite the formation of four provincial party committees, the first to be formed since the Cultural Revolution. Its call for unity and organizational discipline, reiterating a theme first issued at the Ninth Party Congress in April 1969, and its appeal to senior cadres to follow Mao's revolutionary line "still better," attest to the complexity of personnel and policy problems still plaguing party building and to the regime's frustrations over continued political squabbling in some locales.*

The editorial's stock-taking of improvements in Peking's international position is surprisingly limited. It pointedly ignores China's achievements in the diplomatic field, such as recognition from Canada and Italy and the favorable UN vote. Instead, it trots out Peking's favorite "betes noires"--US-Soviet collusion and Japanese militarism--as well as examples which allegedly bear out Mao's statement on 2 May that revolution is the sign of the times. As in last year's editorial, Moscow's revisionist policies are declared to be bankrupt, but this time recent events in Poland are cited to point up the "deep crisis" in Eastern Europe.

Although the New Year statement is vague on the timing of the National People's Congress, which is expected to serve as a forum for unveiling the central government apparatus and a new five-year plan, the editorial struck a positive note in announcing that 1971 would be the first year of the Fourth Five-Year Plan. Predictions for the economy were even more modest than last year, however, and there were no claims that current planning would generate another "great leap forward."

1

Declassified in Part - Sanitized Copy Approved for Release 2016/07/19 : CIA-RDP79T00936A009100020001-4

Declassified in Part - Sanitized Copy Approved for Release 2016/07/19 : CIA-RDP79T00936A009100020001-4

50X1

50X1

50X1

50X1

50X1

2

Declassified in Part - Sanitized Copy Approved for Release 2016/07/19 : CIA-RDP79T00936A009100020001-4

Declassified in Part - Sanitized Copy Approved for Release 2016/07/19 : CIA-RDP79T00936A009100020001-4

VENEZUELA

The secretary general of the governing party said at a press conference this week that the Organization of American States should allow governments to re-establish relations with Cuba if they want to do so. This could be done, he said, now that "Castro has changed his conduct with regard to the interference in the internal affairs of other countries." Earlier, the Venezuelans had suggested that Trinidad's Prime Minister Williams explore the possibility of a rapprochement with Cuba, saying that Venezuela would follow Trinidad's lead.

These are only tentative moves, but they suggest Venezuela is considering seriously steps that could be taken to bring Cuba into the inter-American system. Caracas played an important role in the 1963 OAS decision to isolate Cuba and has steadfastly backed this policy since. A change of Venezuelan policy could prompt several Latin countries to follow suit.

3

Declassified in Part - Sanitized Copy Approved for Release 2016/07/19 : CIA-RDP79T00936A009100020001-4

Declassified in Part - Sanitized Copy Approved for Release 2016/07/19 : CIA-RDP79T00936A009100020001-4

50X1
50X1

Declassified in Part - Sanitized Copy Approved for Release 2016/07/19 : CIA-RDP79T00936A009100020001-4

Declassified in Part - Sanitized Copy Approved for Release 2016/07/19 : CIA-RDP79T00936A009100020001-4

NOTE

Laos: In northern Laos, an estimated 200 enemy troops have attacked elements of a government irregular battalion deployed about eight miles north of Ban Ban. There were no government casualties, but the irregulars were forced to withdraw to the north and east. In addition, late reports indicate that enemy forces yesterday overran several government outposts about seven miles northwest of Ban Ban. In the south, enemy attacks forced the abandonment on 1 January of three small sites on the southern rim of the Bolovens Plateau, which had been manned by some 200 locally recruited irregulars.

4

Declassified in Part - Sanitized Copy Approved for Release 2016/07/19 : CIA-RDP79T00936A009100020001-4

Declassified in Part - Sanitized Copy Approved for Release 2016/07/19 : CIA-RDP79T00936A009100020001-4

Top Secret

Declassified in Part - Sanitized Copy Approved for Release 2016/07/19 : CIA-RDP79T00936A009100020001-4

Declassified in Part - Sanitized Copy Approved for Release 2016/07/19 : CIA-RDP79T00936A009100030001-3

The President's Daily Brief

4 January 1971

25

Top Secret

50X1

Declassified in Part - Sanitized Copy Approved for Release 2016/07/19 : CIA-RDP79T00936A009100030001-3

Declassified in Part - Sanitized Copy Approved for Release 2016/07/19 : CIA-RDP79T00936A009100030001-3

THE PRESIDENT'S DAILY BRIEF

4 January 1971

PRINCIPAL DEVELOPMENTS

Part of the Cambodian Government force trying to open Route 4 southwest of the capital was ambushed over the weekend. *(Page 1)*

In Laos, government irregulars moving on Ban Ban from the north have been forced to pull back from several positions in the past few days. *(Page 2)*

Kosygin's interview with a Japanese newspaper, in which he reiterated Soviet endorsement of SALT, has been given some play in Soviet news media. *(Page 3)*

Fedayeen

50X1

(Page 4)

In Bolivia, Torres' promise of elections may undercut some critics who have been plotting against him. *(Page 5)*

Declassified in Part - Sanitized Copy Approved for Release 2016/07/19 : CIA-RDP79T00936A009100030001-3

Declassified in Part - Sanitized Copy Approved for Release 2016/07/19 : CIA-RDP79T00936A009100030001-3

50X1
50X1

Declassified in Part - Sanitized Copy Approved for Release 2016/07/19 : CIA-RDP79T00936A009100030001-3

Declassified in Part - Sanitized Copy Approved for Release 2016/07/19 : CIA-RDP79T00936A009100030001-3

CAMBODIA

Government troops moving from the south on 1 January to retake the Pich Nil pass area on Route 4 were ambushed and routed by Communist forces about 14 miles north of Veal Renh. Part of the task force regrouped to the south at Taney village, but was again attacked by a large enemy force which also destroyed a bridge on the highway. The next day the remainder of the task force was attacked just north of Taney.

50X1

50X1

50X1

The government's plans to reopen Route 4 may be stalled by these setbacks, although government units approaching the Pich Nil pass from the north have so far proceeded without incident.

50X1

50X1

50X1

1

Declassified in Part - Sanitized Copy Approved for Release 2016/07/19 : CIA-RDP79T00936A009100030001-3

Declassified in Part - Sanitized Copy Approved for Release 2016/07/19 : CIA-RDP79T00936A009100030001-3

50X1
50X1

Declassified in Part - Sanitized Copy Approved for Release 2016/07/19 : CIA-RDP79T00936A009100030001-3

Declassified in Part - Sanitized Copy Approved for Release 2016/07/19 : CIA-RDP79T00936A009100030001-3

LAOS

Between 31 December and 3 January the Communists attacked a total of ten government irregular positions northwest and northeast of Ban Ban. In each action the irregulars withdrew to the north and allowed the position to fall rather than risk unacceptably high casualties.

> *This spate of attacks seems to indicate stiffer enemy resistance to the harassing operation by several battalions of Vang Pao's irregulars against the Communist logistics base at Ban Ban.*

50X1

On the Plaine's western flank, there was little weekend combat activity although the irregular-neutralist base at Muong Soui received two light rocket attacks.

50X1

In southern Laos, government irregulars have retaken without opposition two of the three small sites on the southern rim of the Bolovens Plateau that fell to the enemy on 1 January. In addition, Site 22, the last major government base on the plateau's eastern rim, came under mortar attack on 3 January, but there were no casualties.

2

Declassified in Part - Sanitized Copy Approved for Release 2016/07/19 : CIA-RDP79T00936A009100030001-3

Declassified in Part - Sanitized Copy Approved for Release 2016/07/19 : CIA-RDP79T00936A009100030001-3

USSR

Premier Kosygin reiterated Moscow's endorsement of SALT in an interview with a Japanese newspaper on 1 January which has been published, at least in part, by the Soviet news agency TASS and by Izvestia. We have not received the full Izvestia account, but in the TASS version Kosygin expressed the Soviet desire for "reasonable" agreement equally advantageous to both sides. He said "a study of relevant questions" continued during the last session at Helsinki, but added that these problems are not simple and that positive results require efforts by both sides.

> *Kosygin expressed similar views in an interview with an Indian journalist last August, but his comments were not repeated in the Soviet news media. Brezhnev's remarks on this subject were given wide press coverage last April when he said the USSR would welcome a "sensible" agreement and would do its utmost to make the SALT talks useful.*

3

Declassified in Part - Sanitized Copy Approved for Release 2016/07/19 : CIA-RDP79T00936A009100030001-3

Declassified in Part - Sanitized Copy Approved for Release 2016/07/19 : CIA-RDP79T00936A009100030001-3

FEDAYEEN

50X1

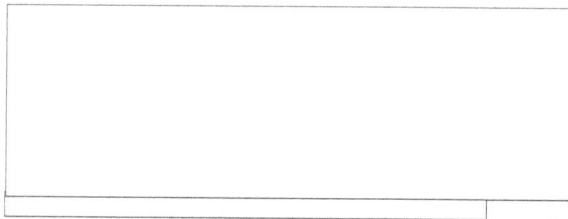

50X1

50X1

4

Declassified in Part - Sanitized Copy Approved for Release 2016/07/19 : CIA-RDP79T00936A009100030001-3

Declassified in Part - Sanitized Copy Approved for Release 2016/07/19 : CIA-RDP79T00936A009100030001-3

NOTE

Bolivia: Eight military officers who took part in the overthrow last October of former President Ovando have been relieved of their commands, and two members of the three-man military junta named shortly before President Torres assumed power have been retired. In addition, Torres has announced that he will call elections as soon as a nationwide referendum scheduled for June approves a new constitution and electoral statutes.

50X1
50X1

50X1

5

Declassified in Part - Sanitized Copy Approved for Release 2016/07/19 : CIA-RDP79T00936A009100030001-3

Declassified in Part - Sanitized Copy Approved for Release 2016/07/19 : CIA-RDP79T00936A009100030001-3

Top Secret

Declassified in Part - Sanitized Copy Approved for Release 2016/07/19 : CIA-RDP79T00936A009100030001-3

Declassified in Part - Sanitized Copy Approved for Release 2016/07/19 : CIA-RDP79T00936A009100040001-2

The President's Daily Brief

5 January 1971

46

Top Secret 50X1

Declassified in Part - Sanitized Copy Approved for Release 2016/07/19 : CIA-RDP79T00936A009100040001-2

Declassified in Part - Sanitized Copy Approved for Release 2016/07/19 : CIA-RDP79T00936A009100040001-2

THE PRESIDENT'S DAILY BRIEF

5 January 1971

PRINCIPAL DEVELOPMENTS

[   ] Cambodian troops   50X1
clear Route 4.   *(Page 1)*

Romania's efforts to remain independent of the USSR
have been enhanced by a long-term, interest-free
credit from China.   *(Page 2)*

On *Page 3* [   ]   50X1
[   ] East German [   ]   50X11
[   ]   50X1

Declassified in Part - Sanitized Copy Approved for Release 2016/07/19 : CIA-RDP79T00936A009100040001-2

Declassified in Part - Sanitized Copy Approved for Release 2016/07/19 : CIA-RDP79T00936A009100040001-2

Current Situation

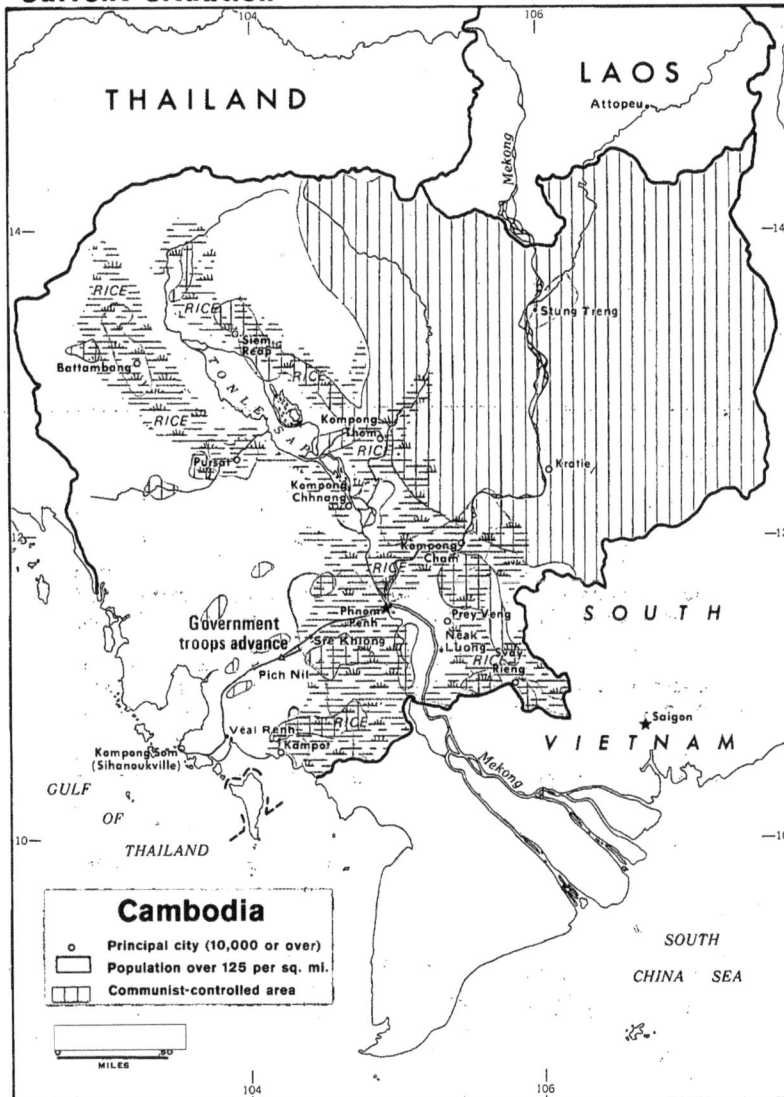

THAILAND

LAOS

Attopeu

Mekong

RICE

RICE

Siem Reap

Battambong

TONLE SAP

RICE

Stung Treng

Kompong Thom

RICE

Pursat

Kratie

Kompong Chhnang

Kompong Cham

RICE

SOUTH

Government troops advance

Phnom Penh

Prey Veng

Neak Luong

Sre Khlong

RICE

Svay Rieng

Pich Nil

Saigon

Veal Renh

RICE

VIETNAM

Kampot

Kompong Som (Sihanoukville)

GULF

OF

THAILAND

SOUTH

CHINA SEA

Mekong

Cambodia

o Principal city (10,000 or over)

▢ Population over 125 per sq. mi.

▣ Communist-controlled area

MILES

50X1

550780 1-71 CIA

Declassified in Part - Sanitized Copy Approved for Release 2016/07/19 : CIA-RDP79T00936A009100040001-2

Declassified in Part - Sanitized Copy Approved for Release 2016/07/19 : CIA-RDP79T00936A009100040001-2

CAMBODIA - SOUTH VIETNAM

50X1

50X1

50X1

50X1

Yesterday Cambodian forces moved westward along Route 4 from Sre Khlong to within ten miles of the Pich Nil pass without opposition. Southwest of the pass, however, Cambodian troops are still in disarray, following the rout last weekend of a three-battalion government task force north of Veal Renh.

50X1

50X1

1

Declassified in Part - Sanitized Copy Approved for Release 2016/07/19 : CIA-RDP79T00936A009100040001-2

Declassified in Part - Sanitized Copy Approved for Release 2016/07/19 : CIA-RDP79T00936A009100040001-2

COMMUNIST CHINA - ROMANIA

The Romanian ambassador in Washington says that the long-term, interest-free credit extended Bucharest by Peking last November amounts to $100 million in convertible currency.

50X1

50X1

50X1

A $100-million cash loan would be the largest China has ever extended. It comes at an appropriate time for the Romanians, who face substantial repayment commitments to a number of countries over the next several years. The Soviets will take further umbrage at this latest instance of Romanian independence, but Bucharest believes the economic benefits outweigh the credit's political risks.

2

Declassified in Part - Sanitized Copy Approved for Release 2016/07/19 : CIA-RDP79T00936A009100040001-2

Declassified in Part - Sanitized Copy Approved for Release 2016/07/19 : CIA-RDP79T00936A009100040001-2

EAST GERMANY

In a major speech last month Premier Stoph told the central committee plenum that East Germany's economic growth rate from 1969 to 1970 was six percent per annum. Stoph has since been contradicted by an economist, Juergen Kuczynski, who wrote an article in <u>Neues Deutschland</u>, the main party daily, which said the growth rate was four percent.

50X1

50X1

50X1

3

Declassified in Part - Sanitized Copy Approved for Release 2016/07/19 : CIA-RDP79T00936A009100040001-2

Declassified in Part - Sanitized Copy Approved for Release 2016/07/19 : CIA-RDP79T00936A009100040001-2

Top Secret

Declassified in Part - Sanitized Copy Approved for Release 2016/07/19 : CIA-RDP79T00936A009100040001-2

Declassified in Part - Sanitized Copy Approved for Release 2016/07/19 : CIA-RDP79T00936A009100050001-1

The President's Daily Brief

6 January 1971

14

Top Secret 50X1

Declassified in Part - Sanitized Copy Approved for Release 2016/07/19 : CIA-RDP79T00936A009100050001-1

Declassified in Part - Sanitized Copy Approved for Release 2016/07/19 : CIA-RDP79T00936A009100050001-1

THE PRESIDENT'S DAILY BRIEF

6 January 1971

PRINCIPAL DEVELOPMENTS

Vietnam _____ South *(Page 1)*   50X1
50X1
50X1

_____ Vietnam _____ *(Page 2)*   50X1
50X1

The Communists have opened a new road in the Laotian panhandle. *(Page 3)*

_____ *(Page 4)*   50X1
50X1

Soviet ___ Guinea ___ Page 5.   50X1
50X1

50X1

(Page 6)   50X1

Declassified in Part - Sanitized Copy Approved for Release 2016/07/19 : CIA-RDP79T00936A009100050001-1

SOUTH VIETNAM

50X1
50X1
50X1

50X1
50X1

50X1
50X1

50X1
50X1

50X1
50X1

50X1
50X1

50X1

1

North Vietnam: Infiltration Starts

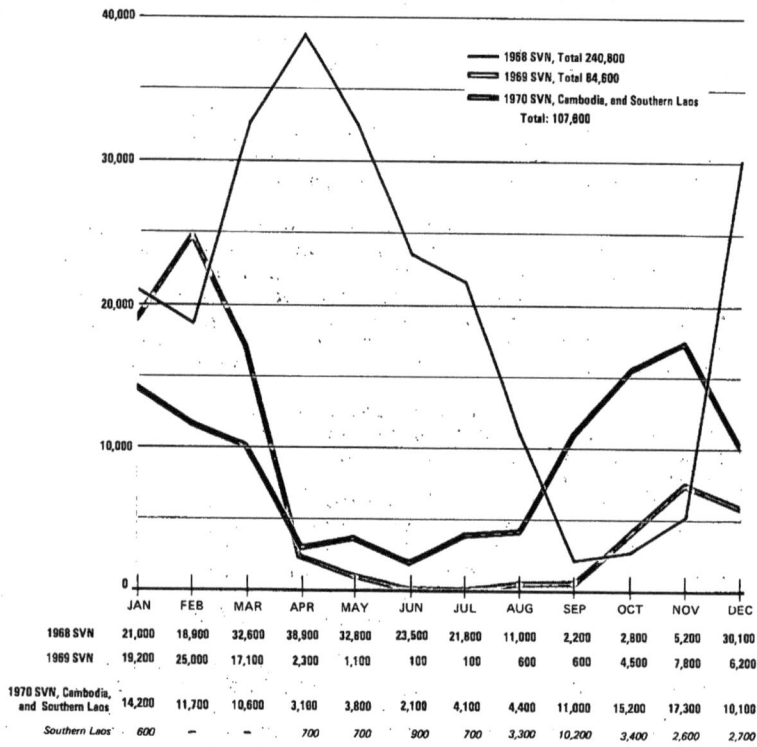

Legend:
- 1968 SVN, Total 240,800
- 1969 SVN, Total 84,600
- 1970 SVN, Cambodia, and Southern Laos Total: 107,800

	JAN	FEB	MAR	APR	MAY	JUN	JUL	AUG	SEP	OCT	NOV	DEC
1968 SVN	21,000	18,900	32,600	38,900	32,800	23,500	21,800	11,000	2,200	2,800	5,200	30,100
1969 SVN	19,200	25,000	17,100	2,300	1,100	100	100	600	600	4,500	7,800	6,200
1970 SVN, Cambodia, and Southern Laos	14,200	11,700	10,600	3,100	3,800	2,100	4,100	4,400	11,000	15,200	17,300	10,100
Southern Laos	600	—	—	700	700	900	700	3,300	10,200	3,400	2,600	2,700

Totals for 1968 and 1969 include troops bound for South Vietnam only; those for 1970 include troops bound for South Vietnam, Southern Laos, and Cambodia.

550781 1-71 CIA

50X1

Declassified in Part - Sanitized Copy Approved for Release 2016/07/19 : CIA-RDP79T00936A009100050001-1

VIETNAM

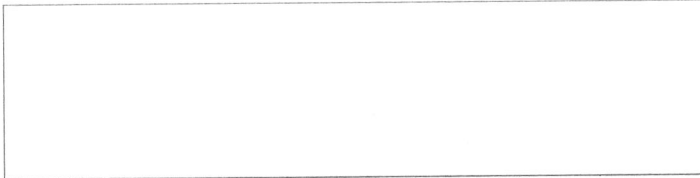

50X1

50X1

50X1

2

Declassified in Part - Sanitized Copy Approved for Release 2016/07/19 : CIA-RDP79T00936A009100050001-1

Declassified in Part - Sanitized Copy Approved for Release 2016/07/19 : CIA-RDP79T00936A009100050001-1

LAOS: New major road construction

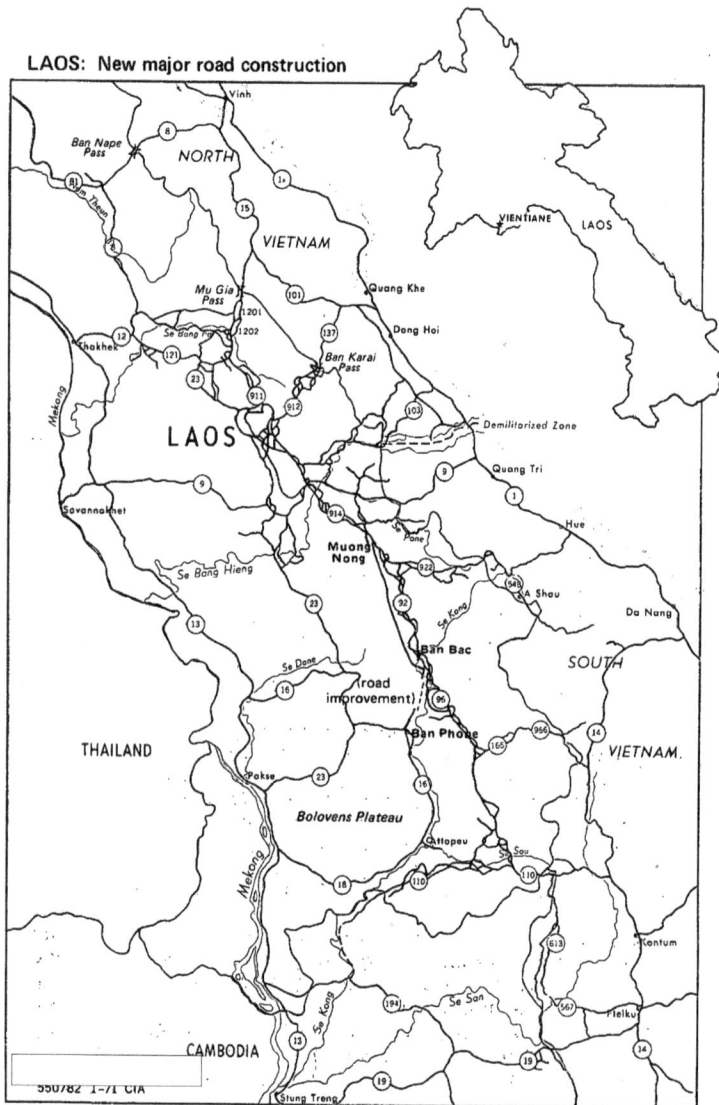

550782 1-71 CIA

50X1

Declassified in Part - Sanitized Copy Approved for Release 2016/07/19 : CIA-RDP79T00936A009100050001-1

Declassified in Part - Sanitized Copy Approved for Release 2016/07/19 : CIA-RDP79T00936A009100050001-1

LAOS

Recent photography [   ] indicate
that the Communists have opened a new 70-mile road
from Muong Nong to a point on the Se Kong River
about 15 miles south of Ban Bac. It parallels a
heavily bombed stretch of Routes 92 and 96, the
main north-south road. According to intercepts,
additional engineering units have been shifted to
the new road, and air observers report that construction of AAA sites is under way. The Communists are also improving and constructing roads
in the area between Ban Bac and Ban Phone close
to the Bolovens Plateau.

50X1

> *The new road presumably is intended to
> lessen the effects of the US bombing pro-
> gram and to increase the flow of supplies
> to extreme southern Laos and Cambodia.
> The Communists have also taken steps to
> open a westerly alternate to the main
> north-south route via Routes 23 and 16,
> but it is unlikely that these routes
> will assume a heavy logistic burden un-
> less government forces are driven from
> the Bolovens Plateau, the dominant stra-
> tegic terrain in southwestern Laos.*

3

Declassified in Part - Sanitized Copy Approved for Release 2016/07/19 : CIA-RDP79T00936A009100050001-1

Declassified in Part - Sanitized Copy Approved for Release 2016/07/19 : CIA-RDP79T00936A009100050001-1

FEDAYEEN

 50X1

 50X1
50X1

 50X1

 50X1

4

Declassified in Part - Sanitized Copy Approved for Release 2016/07/19 : CIA-RDP79T00936A009100050001-1

Declassified in Part - Sanitized Copy Approved for Release 2016/07/19 : CIA-RDP79T00936A009100050001-1

USSR-GUINEA

 50X1

 50X1

 50X1

 50X1

 50X1

50X1 50X1

 50X1

5

Declassified in Part - Sanitized Copy Approved for Release 2016/07/19 : CIA-RDP79T00936A009100050001-1

Declassified in Part - Sanitized Copy Approved for Release 2016/07/19 : CIA-RDP79T00936A009100050001-1

NOTES

USSR-Cuba:    50X1X1

USSR: Moscow has announced that last year's grain crop was 185 million tons, surpassing the previous high of 171 million tons harvested in 1966. The 1970 harvest should yield a usable output of about 150 million tons, approximately 15 percent above the average level achieved in 1966-69 and ample to meet domestic needs and foreign commitments. The harvest will increase feed supplies and eventually should alleviate the meat shortage of the past two years.

6

Declassified in Part - Sanitized Copy Approved for Release 2016/07/19 : CIA-RDP79T00936A009100050001-1

Declassified in Part - Sanitized Copy Approved for Release 2016/07/19 : CIA-RDP79T00936A009100050001-1

Top Secret

Declassified in Part - Sanitized Copy Approved for Release 2016/07/19 : CIA-RDP79T00936A009100050001-1

Declassified in Part - Sanitized Copy Approved for Release 2016/06/14 : CIA-RDP79T00936A009100060001-0

The President's Daily Brief

7 *January 1971*

47

Top Secret 50X1

Declassified in Part - Sanitized Copy Approved for Release 2016/06/14 : CIA-RDP79T00936A009100060001-0

Declassified in Part - Sanitized Copy Approved for Release 2016/06/14 : CIA-RDP79T00936A009100060001-0

THE PRESIDENT'S DAILY BRIEF

7 January 1971

PRINCIPAL DEVELOPMENTS

There are some signs that the Communists plan a new round of attacks in South Vietnam in the middle of this month, especially in the northern provinces. *(Page 1)*

In Laos, government irregulars have ended their harassing operation against Ban Ban. *(Page 2)*

The Soviets appear to have started only one SA-5 complex during 1970. *(Page 3)*

At Annex, we appraise the attitude of the Egyptian military as it affects the Sadat regime's approach to the Jarring talks.

Declassified in Part - Sanitized Copy Approved for Release 2016/06/14 : CIA-RDP79T00936A009100060001-0

Declassified in Part - Sanitized Copy Approved for Release 2016/06/14 : CIA-RDP79T00936A009100060001-0

Declassified in Part - Sanitized Copy Approved for Release 2016/06/14 : CIA-RDP79T00936A009100060001-0

Declassified in Part - Sanitized Copy Approved for Release 2016/06/14 : CIA-RDP79T00936A009100060001-0

SOUTH VIETNAM

There are signs that the Communists plan a new round of attacks in mid-January, especially in the northern half of the country. Intercepts show that several North Vietnamese infantry and artillery units in the eastern DMZ area and in the northern provinces of Thua Thien and Quang Nam are either combat-ready or are preparing for tactical operations.

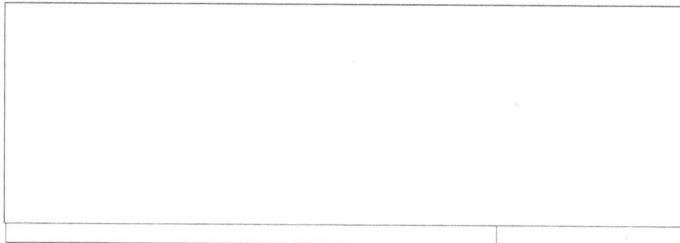

50X1

50X1

The projected attacks, while of greater scope than those of the past several months, will probably be for the most part the familiar mixture of shellings, small-scale ground attacks, and terrorism. In the southern part of the country, the contemplated enemy offensive seems to be on a much more restricted scale than in the north, presumably because operations in Cambodia have forced the Communists to curtail their efforts around Saigon and in the delta.

1

Declassified in Part - Sanitized Copy Approved for Release 2016/06/14 : CIA-RDP79T00936A009100060001-0

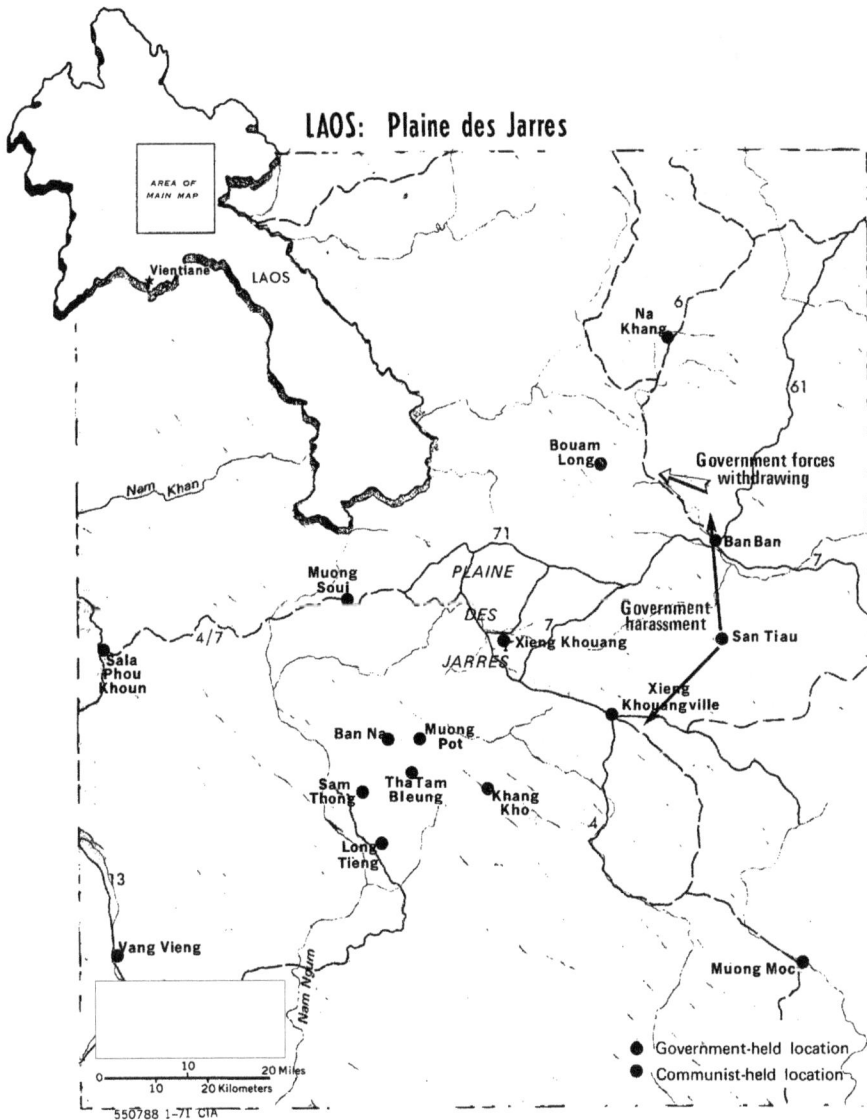

Declassified in Part - Sanitized Copy Approved for Release 2016/06/14 : CIA-RDP79T00936A009100060001-0

LAOS: Plaine des Jarres

AREA OF
MAIN MAP

Vientiane
LAOS

Na
Khang

6

61

Bouam
Long

Government forces
withdrawing

Nam Khan

71

Ban Ban

7

PLAINE

Muong
Soui

DES

Government
harassment

4/7

7
Xieng Khouang

San Tiau

Sala
Phou
Khoun

JARRES

Xieng
Khouangville

Ban Na

Muong
Pot

Sam
Thong

Tha Tam
Bleung

Khang
Kho

4

Long
Tieng

13

Vang Vieng

Muong Moc

50X1

0   10   20 Miles
0 10   20 Kilometers

● Government-held location
● Communist-held location

550788 1-7T CIA

Declassified in Part - Sanitized Copy Approved for Release 2016/06/14 : CIA-RDP79T00936A009100060001-0

Declassified in Part - Sanitized Copy Approved for Release 2016/06/14 : CIA-RDP79T00936A009100060001-0

LAOS

Government irregulars have terminated their six-week harassing operation against Ban Ban and have withdrawn from the immediate area. The four battalions south of Ban Ban will undertake other harassing missions, while the three to the north are now returning to the vicinity of Bouam Long.

The operation was beset by bad weather, lackluster leadership, and unavoidable delays which resulted in the loss of surprise. It failed to achieve a primary objective--penetrating the Ban Ban Valley to harass enemy logistic operations there-- but did destroy small stockpiles nearby. The cost in casualties was relatively light.

The operation, which forced the Communists to divert a North Vietnamese battalion from the western Plaine des Jarres to the defense of Ban Ban, did help to keep the North Vietnamese away from the irregular bases on the Plaine's western edge. The Communists were unable to mount any substantial offensive toward Long Tieng even though they were clearly aware of the opportunities afforded by the depletion of government strength in the region.

The longer term consequences of the Ban Ban operation are less clear. Its principal effect may have been to delay an anticipated enemy push toward Long Tieng. The withdrawal from the Plaine last summer of the North Vietnamese 312th Division and the opening of preliminary talks between the Lao Communists and the government may have meant that Hanoi preferred to defer a major offensive in north Laos this year. There are indications, however, that the 312th may now be returning, possibly even in reaction to the Ban Ban operation. Its return would increase the possibility of a repetition of last year's Communist offensive against Long Tieng.

2

Declassified in Part - Sanitized Copy Approved for Release 2016/06/14 : CIA-RDP79T00936A009100060001-0

50X1

50X1

50X1

Declassified in Part - Sanitized Copy Approved for Release 2016/06/14 : CIA-RDP79T00936A009100060001-0

USSR

Satellite photography of most of the areas where additional SA-5 (long-range surface-to-air missile at one time known as the "Tallinn system") site construction had been expected shows only one new complex started during 1970.

50X1

3

Declassified in Part - Sanitized Copy Approved for Release 2016/06/14 : CIA-RDP79T00936A009100060001-0

EGYPT AND THE JARRING TALKS

The reactivation of the mission of UN negotiator Jarring provides another breathing space in the dead-locked situation in the Middle East but does not sig-nificantly ameliorate the immediate problems con-fronting the Egyptian regime. In facing these prob-lems, the Sadat regime will be influenced to a great degree by the attitudes of the military, since the military virtually alone possess the means to force change in the country's leadership.

A precise reading of the attitudes of the various segments of Egyptian society toward the struggle with Israel and the cease-fire is difficult. The problem is compounded when attempting to assess the mood of the armed forces because of the isolation of military personnel from Western observers.

Thus, it is likely that Egyptian policy over the next few months will be influenced by the more militant atti-tudes within the armed forces, or at least by anxiety among Sadat and his immediate advisers that elements

50X1
50X1

50X1

50X1

50X1
50X1

50X1

A1.

ANNEX

Declassified in Part - Sanitized Copy Approved for Release 2016/06/14 : CIA-RDP79T00936A009100060001-0

in the military might use any "blunder" in the negotiations to undercut the regime. Additionally,
Sadat may feel compelled to prove he is as militant
as Nasir was in opposition to Israel. This will
tend to make Egyptian policy less than forthcoming
and add to the already formidable problems facing
Jarring.

To arm itself psychologically on both the diplomatic
and the domestic fronts, the Sadat regime is devoting
a large volume of rhetoric to the "battle" with Israel. Echoing some of Nasir's pronouncements, Sadat
recently has been stressing the need for military
and civilian preparedness.

50X1

50X1

50X1

Sadat has also attempted privately to convince us
that he is serious when he declares publicly that
Egypt will not agree to extend the cease-fire unless
"there is a definite timetable for withdrawal" of
Israeli forces.

50X1

50X1

There is, nonetheless, little sign at this point
that Sadat and company are becoming prisoners of
their own posturing in the way that Nasir did before
the 1967 war. At the moment, the sound and fury
amounts largely to pressure tactics. Without something it can sell as "progress," however, the Egyptian leadership is still capable of trapping itself
into a situation where any action, regardless of
how obviously disastrous its ultimate result might
be, would seem preferable to impotent passivity in
the face of an unyielding Israel.

A2

Declassified in Part - Sanitized Copy Approved for Release 2016/06/14 : CIA-RDP79T00936A009100060001-0

Declassified in Part - Sanitized Copy Approved for Release 2016/06/14 : CIA-RDP79T00936A009100060001-0

Top Secret

Declassified in Part - Sanitized Copy Approved for Release 2016/06/14 : CIA-RDP79T00936A009100060001-0

Declassified in Part - Sanitized Copy Approved for Release 2016/06/14 : CIA-RDP79T00936A009100070001-9

The President's Daily Brief

8 *January* 1971

49

~~Top Secret~~ 50X1

Declassified in Part - Sanitized Copy Approved for Release 2016/06/14 : CIA-RDP79T00936A009100070001-9

Declassified in Part - Sanitized Copy Approved for Release 2016/06/14 : CIA-RDP79T00936A009100070001-9

THE PRESIDENT'S DAILY BRIEF

8 January 1971

PRINCIPAL DEVELOPMENTS

Preliminary indications are that the Israelis intend to stick to a tough negotiating position in their current talks with Jarring. *(Page 1)*

Petroleum stocks in Phnom Penh are dwindling rapidly. *(Page 2)*

On *Page 3* ⬚⬚⬚⬚⬚⬚⬚⬚⬚⬚⬚⬚⬚⬚⬚⬚⬚⬚   50X1
⬚⬚⬚ Chinese Communist ⬚⬚⬚⬚⬚⬚⬚⬚⬚   50X1
⬚⬚⬚⬚⬚⬚⬚⬚⬚⬚⬚⬚⬚⬚⬚⬚.   50X1

Reports of further labor trouble in Poland are discussed on *Page 4*.

⬚⬚⬚⬚⬚⬚⬚⬚⬚⬚⬚⬚⬚⬚⬚⬚⬚⬚⬚⬚⬚⬚   50X1
⬚⬚⬚⬚⬚⬚⬚⬚⬚⬚⬚⬚⬚⬚⬚⬚⬚ *(Page 5)*   50X1

Declassified in Part - Sanitized Copy Approved for Release 2016/06/14 : CIA-RDP79T00936A009100070001-9

Declassified in Part - Sanitized Copy Approved for Release 2016/06/14 : CIA-RDP79T00936A009100070001-9

ISRAEL

Foreign Minister Eban gave Ambassador Barbour a memorandum on Wednesday reiterating all of Israel's established positions and stating flatly that no Israeli troops will be withdrawn from any position pending an over-all settlement, that Israel will not return to its pre - June 1967 boundaries, and that Jerusalem will "of course" remain the capital of Israel, though with arrangements for "safeguarding universal spiritual interests."

Eban made it clear when presenting the aide memoire that the Israelis are not willing to enter serious talks on substantive problems unless the Egyptians stop creating an "ultimative situation"-- i.e., stop threatening not to renew the cease-fire after 5 February. Eban even said he was considering telling Jarring that a further extension of the cease-fire is a condition for Israel's continuation of the talks.

> *If Prime Minister Meir takes a line as bluntly tough as this in her current talks with Jarring, he will in effect return to New York worse than empty-handed. Barring some unforeseen break in the situation, such a development would bring an Egyptian call for a fresh meeting of the Security Council at an early date.*

1

Declassified in Part - Sanitized Copy Approved for Release 2016/06/14 : CIA-RDP79T00936A009100070001-9

Declassified in Part - Sanitized Copy Approved for Release 2016/06/14 : CIA-RDP79T00936A009100070001-9

Declassified in Part - Sanitized Copy Approved for Release 2016/06/14 : CIA-RDP79T00936A009100070001-9

Declassified in Part - Sanitized Copy Approved for Release 2016/06/14 : CIA-RDP79T00936A009100070001-9

CAMBODIA

Phnom Penh's supplies of fuel oil and kerosene, primarily for civilian use, are nearly depleted. Lon Nol intends to restrict the use of petroleum products to ensure the continued operation of electric generating plants and other essential facilities, which may otherwise be forced to shut down before the end of the month. In military stocks there is a two-week supply of aviation gas and about one month's supply of gasoline for vehicles.

The shortage has been brought about by the closure since late November of Route 4, which links Phnom Penh with Cambodia's only oil refinery and deep-water seaport, and by the recent ambushes of petroleum convoys on the Mekong River.

The major oil companies have been making emergency riverine deliveries from Saigon to Phnom Penh since mid-December. It is questionable, however, whether crews and ship owners can be persuaded to risk another run up the river in view of recent heavy Communist attacks. Lon Nol is considering steps to increase air support for future river convoys and to mount intensified Cambodian - South Vietnamese ground operations to control river banks between Phnom Penh and the South Vietnam border.

2

Declassified in Part - Sanitized Copy Approved for Release 2016/06/14 : CIA-RDP79T00936A009100070001-9

Declassified in Part - Sanitized Copy Approved for Release 2016/06/14 : CIA-RDP79T00936A009100070001-9

COMMUNIST CHINA

 50X1

 50X1

 50X1

50X1

50X1

50X1

3

Declassified in Part - Sanitized Copy Approved for Release 2016/06/14 : CIA-RDP79T00936A009100070001-9

Declassified in Part - Sanitized Copy Approved for Release 2016/06/14 : CIA-RDP79T00936A009100070001-9

POLAND

The Swedish press reports that shipyard workers in Gdansk are again on strike. The strikers are said to be demanding that 200 workers arrested in the December riots be released, and that party leader Gierek come to Gdansk for discussions. The Polish press has not mentioned the strike, but a Polish official has admitted that shipping has been delayed in Gdansk.

> *The new Polish leaders have emphasized the need to re-establish communications, lost by the Gomulka regime, between the workers and the party, and the workers in Gdansk apparently have taken them up on their promise. Gierek has always had good rapport with labor, but the demands of the shipbuilders present a difficult challenge. Large numbers of those arrested during the rioting have already been released, and it is likely that there is a legitimate case to be made against those who remain in jail.*

Meanwhile, local party meetings have been held throughout the country in preparation for a forth-coming central committee plenum to analyze the causes of the December disorders. These meetings have dealt with restoration of the "Leninist norms of party life," which the departed leaders were ac-cused of ignoring, but current signs of labor un-rest may add a new dimension to the plenum.

4

Declassified in Part - Sanitized Copy Approved for Release 2016/06/14 : CIA-RDP79T00936A009100070001-9

Declassified in Part - Sanitized Copy Approved for Release 2016/06/14 : CIA-RDP79T00936A009100070001-9

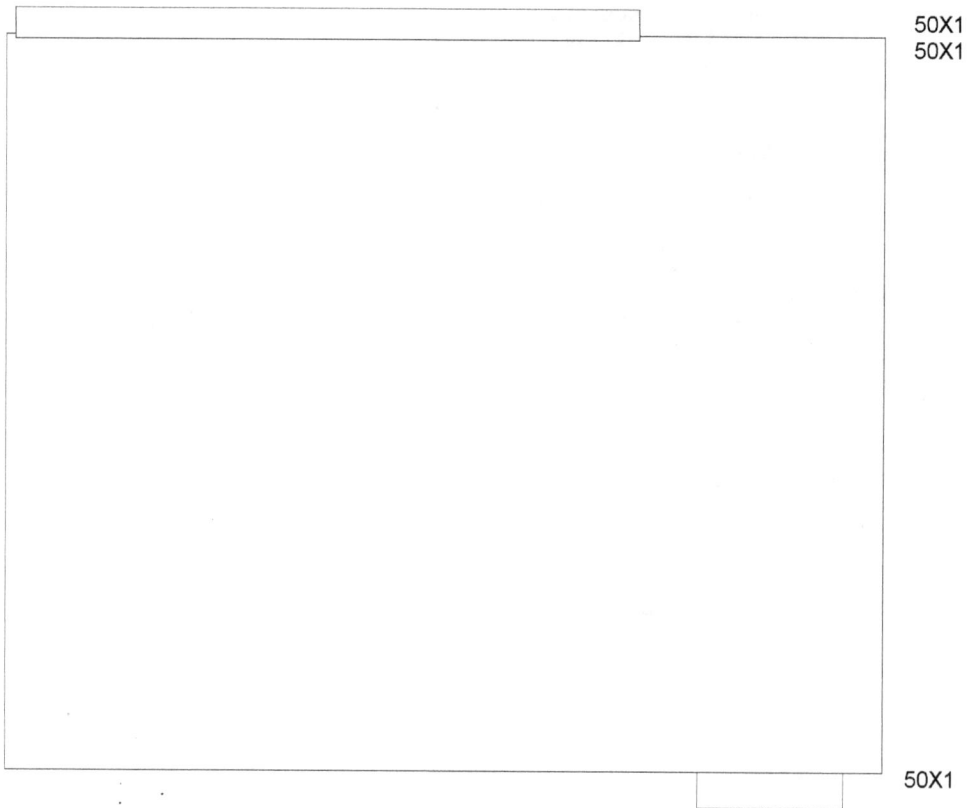

50X1
50X1

50X1

Declassified in Part - Sanitized Copy Approved for Release 2016/06/14 : CIA-RDP79T00936A009100070001-9

Declassified in Part - Sanitized Copy Approved for Release 2016/06/14 : CIA-RDP79T00936A009100070001-9

FOR THE PRESIDENT ONLY

50X1

50X1

50X1

50X1

50X1

50X1

50X1

50X1

5

FOR THE PRESIDENT ONLY

Declassified in Part - Sanitized Copy Approved for Release 2016/06/14 : CIA-RDP79T00936A009100070001-9

Declassified in Part - Sanitized Copy Approved for Release 2016/06/14 : CIA-RDP79T00936A009100070001-9

50X1

Declassified in Part - Sanitized Copy Approved for Release 2016/06/14 : CIA-RDP79T00936A009100070001-9

Declassified in Part - Sanitized Copy Approved for Release 2016/06/14 : CIA-RDP79T00936A009100070001-9

NOTES

Laos: 50X1
                                                                     50X1

                                                                     50X1

Indochina: 50X1
                                                                     50X1

Haiti: The armed forces pledged their support
yesterday to President Duvalier and his son, Jean-
Claude, the heir apparent, in a letter published in
Haitian newspapers. Duvalier has not specifically
named a successor, but he has broadly hinted that
Jean-Claude was his choice. The military apparently
got the message, and declarations of support from
other sectors may soon follow.   50X1
                                                                     50X1
                            if the President should suddenly   50X1
pass from the scene, support for Jean-Claude could
quickly evaporate.

6

Declassified in Part - Sanitized Copy Approved for Release 2016/06/14 : CIA-RDP79T00936A009100070001-9

Declassified in Part - Sanitized Copy Approved for Release 2016/06/14 : CIA-RDP79T00936A009100070001-9

Top Secret

Declassified in Part - Sanitized Copy Approved for Release 2016/06/14 : CIA-RDP79T00936A009100070001-9

Declassified in Part - Sanitized Copy Approved for Release 2016/06/14 : CIA-RDP79T00936A009100080001-8

The President's Daily Brief

9 *January 1971*

47

Top Secret 50X1

Declassified in Part - Sanitized Copy Approved for Release 2016/06/14 : CIA-RDP79T00936A009100080001-8

FOR THE PRESIDENT ONLY

THE PRESIDENT'S DAILY BRIEF

9 January 1971

PRINCIPAL DEVELOPMENTS

Gromyko's protest yesterday against anti-Soviet demonstrations in the United States was unusually blunt. *(Page 1)*

Jordan's army clashed with the fedayeen in several areas yesterday. *(Page 2)*

The military situation in southern Laos is discussed on Page 3.

Uruguayan authorities have not received any demands from the kidnapers of the British ambassador. *(Page 4)*

Industrial and domestic consumers have been hurt by East German power shortages. *(Page 5)*

Declassified in Part - Sanitized Copy Approved for Release 2016/06/14 : CIA-RDP79T00936A009100080001-8

USSR

Gromyko delivered a very strong official protest to Ambassador Beam yesterday against the current anti-Soviet demonstrations in the United States
and Washington's alleged failure to take the necessary measures to stop them. He warned that if the
US did not ensure safe conditions for Soviet officials, the Soviet people may do something that the
US would "not want and may not expect." Gromyko
repeatedly stated that Moscow does not care how the
US may choose to evaluate anything which might hap-
pen from the Soviet side. According to Ambassador
Beam, Gromyko was in a grim mood, and his tone was
unusually blunt. And to punctuate his remarks, the
foreign minister announced at the end of the meeting
that Ambassador Dobrynin would be returning to Moscow "for a brief period" on 10 January.

*This is the most serious demarche that
the Soviets have made regarding the rash
of anti-Soviet incidents in the US. Gromyko's oral protest should not be inter-
preted as less serious than a written
presentation; it appears that time was a
factor. The Soviets seem almost at wit's
end in this matter. The way they see it,
their gradual responses in the face of increasing threats to their official representatives have been to no avail. Almost
certainly, they genuinely believe the US
can stop these attacks. Now, they appear
to be threatening a more striking demon-
strative act.*

*Among their options are a major demonstra-
tion against the US Embassy, an ostenta-
tious postponement of any of a number of
upcoming bilateral talks (or a more pointed
threat of such a step), or some other loud
political gesture. Gromyko's statement
that the Soviets would not care how the
US would evaluate any Soviet move of this
sort, if and when it occurs, is particularly harsh.*

1

Declassified in Part - Sanitized Copy Approved for Release 2016/06/14 : CIA-RDP79T00936A009100080001-8

Declassified in Part - Sanitized Copy Approved for Release 2016/06/14 : CIA-RDP79T00936A009100080001-8

JORDAN: Areas of Fighting

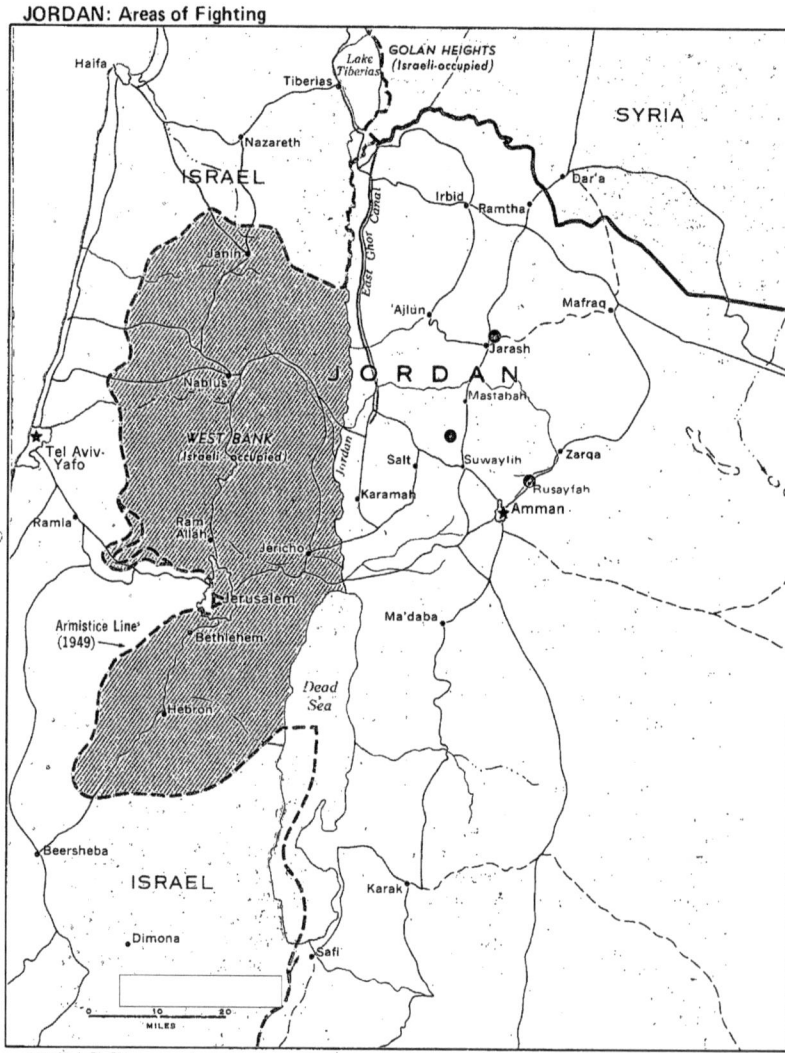

50X1

550802 1-71 CIA

Declassified in Part - Sanitized Copy Approved for Release 2016/06/14 : CIA-RDP79T00936A009100080001-8

Declassified in Part - Sanitized Copy Approved for Release 2016/06/14 : CIA-RDP79T00936A009100080001-8

JORDAN

Early yesterday the Jordanian Army moved against fedayeen centers north and east of Amman. In Rusayfah, about ten miles northeast of the capital, the army claims it blocked a sabotage plot by seizing a cache of arms.

50X1

Later the fighting spread to a hilly part of the Salt-Suwaylih-Mastabah triangle northwest of Amman and continued into the night.

3.5(c)

The Central Committee of the Palestine Liberation Organization was scheduled to meet last night and perhaps again today to develop a coordinated fedayeen position.

> *Decisions reached at these meetings are not likely to control various fedayeen elements that are becoming less and less responsive to leadership. The army also is becoming more inclined to launch independent actions and the departure of cease-fire supervisor Ladgham on Thursday apparently has given the army additional incentive to settle old scores.*

Ladgham is still involved, however, even though he is in Cairo. Yesterday he got in touch with Jordan Premier Tal and asked him to allow observer teams to visit combat areas.

2

Declassified in Part - Sanitized Copy Approved for Release 2016/06/14 : CIA-RDP79T00936A009100080001-8

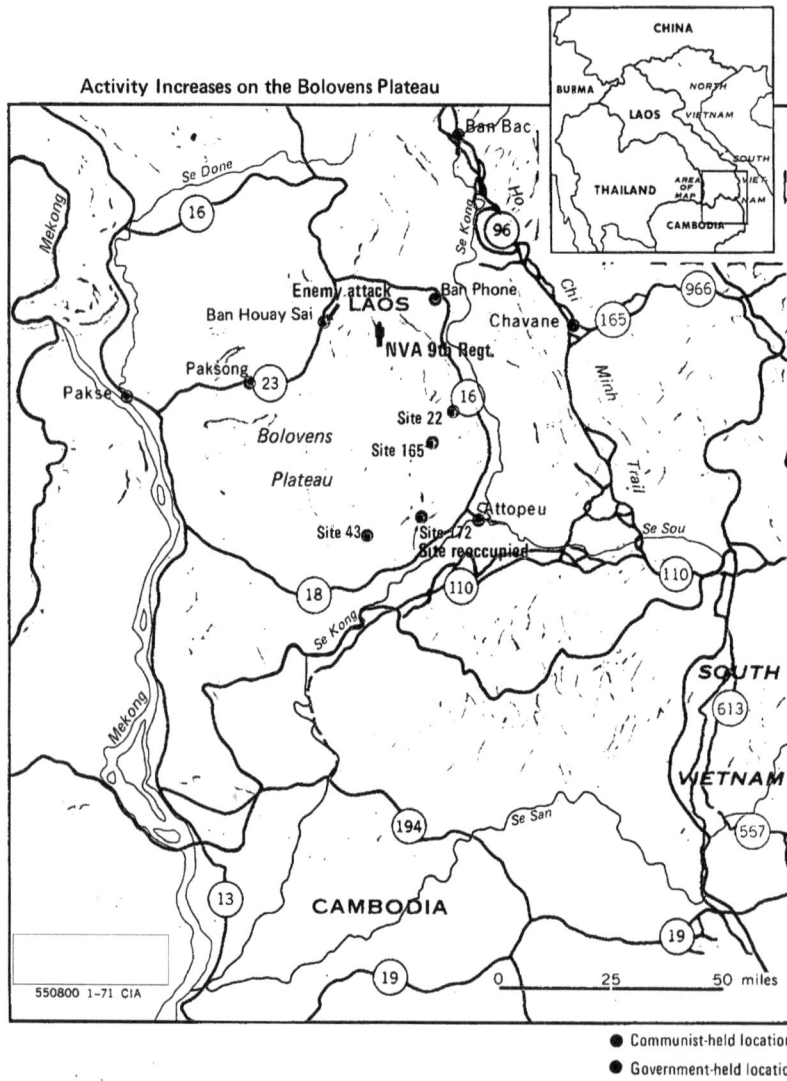

Activity Increases on the Bolovens Plateau

CHINA

BURMA
NORTH
LAOS VIETNAM

THAILAND
AREA
OF
MAP
SOUTH
VIET
NAM

CAMBODIA

Ban Bac

Se Done

16

Se Kong

96

Enemy attack
Ban Houay Sai
Ban Phone
LAOS
Chavane
165
966

NVA 9th Regt.

Paksong
23
16
Pakse
Site 22
Bolovens
Site 165
Plateau

Minh

Trail

Attopeu
Site 43
Site 72
Site reoccupied
Se Sou

18
110
110

Se Kong

SOUTH
613
VIETNAM

194
Se San
557

13
CAMBODIA
19

19
0   25   50 miles

550800 1-71 CIA

50X1

● Communist-held location
● Government-held location

Declassified in Part - Sanitized Copy Approved for Release 2016/06/14 : CIA-RDP79T00936A009100080001-8

LAOS

Military action continues to pick up in the northern and eastern areas of the Bolovens Plateau in southern Laos. Yesterday two newly deployed irregular battalions repulsed a heavy enemy attack against Ban Houay Sai, about 15 miles north of Pak-song. Heavy tactical air support was used to beat back the estimated three-battalion enemy force. Only one irregular was killed, while 116 enemy bodies were found.

> *The attack may have been carried out by elements of the NVA 9th Regiment which moved onto the northern portion of the plateau last month. The size of the assault force suggests that the Communists intend to press southward. The enemy may have concluded that if they can threaten Paksong, the government would pull back from the bases along the eastern rim of the plateau.*

> *We continue to believe that the irregular bases on the eastern rim of the plateau are still the enemy's main target. These bases—especially sites 43, 165, and 22—have been used to launch harassing raids and intelligence gathering operations against the Ho Chi Minh trail.*

Enemy probes and attacks near these positions continue, but in recent weeks the government has improved the defenses of the bases and has brought in fresh reinforcements. On 7 January some of these reinforcements reoccupied Site 172, which had fallen into Communist hands two weeks ago.

3

Declassified in Part - Sanitized Copy Approved for Release 2016/06/14 : CIA-RDP79T00936A009100080001-8

Declassified in Part - Sanitized Copy Approved for Release 2016/06/14 : CIA-RDP79T00936A009100080001-8

URUGUAY

The abduction yesterday of British ambassador Jackson adds a new factor to the case of the kidnaped US agronomist Claude Fly. Together with Brazilian consul Gomide, Fly has been held by the extreme leftist Tupamaros terrorist organization since last summer, when it murdered US AID official Mitrione.

Prospects for Fly's release appeared to be improving earlier this week. A Montevideo daily published the Tupamaros political manifesto, and other papers seemed ready to follow suit. This would have fulfilled the terrorists' demand that the major media publish the document. With Jackson in hand, they may now feel they have more bargaining leverage and so free Fly in the hope of gaining credit for a humanitarian gesture. Until they state their terms for freeing Jackson, however, we cannot be sure how they link the captives' status.

In any event, the Pacheco government is not likely to back off from its refusal to negotiate, a policy which had caused the Tupamaros to scale down their original demands. The terrorists' loss of much public sympathy has convinced Pacheco that his strategy is sound.

50X1

50X1

50X1

4

Declassified in Part - Sanitized Copy Approved for Release 2016/06/14 : CIA-RDP79T00936A009100080001-8

Declassified in Part - Sanitized Copy Approved for Release 2016/06/14 : CIA-RDP79T00936A009100080001-8

NOTE

East Germany: Serious power shortages have temporarily shut down power to some plants and consumers as severe weather persists. Major petrochemical combines have been particularly hard hit by the shortages of electricity, gas, and coal, and the giant Leuna chemical combine may be forced to shut down completely until the situation improves. The populace is accustomed to power failures, which occur almost every winter. Workers in at least one plant, however, are grumbling about salary cuts they are forced to take because their plant is not open a full day.

3.5(c)

5

Declassified in Part - Sanitized Copy Approved for Release 2016/06/14 : CIA-RDP79T00936A009100080001-8

Declassified in Part - Sanitized Copy Approved for Release 2016/06/14 : CIA-RDP79T00936A009100080001-8

Top Secret

Declassified in Part - Sanitized Copy Approved for Release 2016/06/14 : CIA-RDP79T00936A009100080001-8

Declassified in Part - Sanitized Copy Approved for Release 2016/06/14 : CIA-RDP79T00936A009100090001-7

The President's Daily Brief

1 0 JAN 1971

~~11 January~~ 1971

46

Top Secret 50X1

Declassified in Part - Sanitized Copy Approved for Release 2016/06/14 : CIA-RDP79T00936A009100090001-7

Declassified in Part - Sanitized Copy Approved for Release 2016/06/14 : CIA-RDP79T00936A009100090001-7

JORDAN

Fighting has continued into the third day in the north where the army appears to be inflicting heavy casualties on the fedayeen. Only sporadic shooting occurred in Amman, although security force spokesmen claim they will soon clean up trouble spots there. Fedayeen militiamen in refugee camps nearby are preparing for such an attack.

Slowing the army's momentum could become more difficult with the return yesterday of Sharif Nasir, King Husayn's cousin and a hard-line general. The few remaining cease-fire observers announced they were suspending their efforts because of government obstruction.

50X1

50X1

50X1

ILLEGIB

10 JAN 1971

Declassified in Part - Sanitized Copy Approved for Release 2016/06/14 : CIA-RDP79T00936A009100090001-7

Declassified in Part - Sanitized Copy Approved for Release 2016/06/14 : CIA-RDP79T00936A009100090001-7

CAMBODIA

Prime Minister Lon Nol plans to lead a delegation to Saigon on 20 and 21 January. Discussions will cover both military and economic aspects of the South Vietnamese involvement in Cambodia, including Saigon's request that the Cambodians help pay the cost of South Vietnamese participation.

Earlier lower level negotiations foundered on the payments issue, and there is no evidence that either Lon Nol or Thieu is ready to compromise now. The two men met briefly in Cambodia several months ago. If Lon Nol goes ahead with the trip, it will be the first time he has left Cambodia since Sihanouk's ouster last March.

Communist military activity continues low keyed. Light harassment of government forces has been reported in the east along Route 7 and in the southwest along Route 4 near Pich Nil pass.

1 0 JAN 1971

Declassified in Part - Sanitized Copy Approved for Release 2016/06/14 : CIA-RDP79T00936A009100090001-7

Declassified in Part - Sanitized Copy Approved for Release 2016/06/14 : CIA-RDP79T00936A009100090001-7

Top Secret

Declassified in Part - Sanitized Copy Approved for Release 2016/06/14 : CIA-RDP79T00936A009100090001-7

Declassified in Part - Sanitized Copy Approved for Release 2016/06/14 : CIA-RDP79T00936A009100100001-5

The President's Daily Brief

11 January 1971

50

Top Secret 50X1

Declassified in Part - Sanitized Copy Approved for Release 2016/06/14 : CIA-RDP79T00936A009100100001-5

Declassified in Part - Sanitized Copy Approved for Release 2016/06/14 : CIA-RDP79T00936A009100100001-5

THE PRESIDENT'S DAILY BRIEF

11 January 1971

PRINCIPAL DEVELOPMENTS

The Jordanian Army is maintaining heavy pressure on fedayeen centers north of Amman as Arab states seek a new cease-fire. *(Page 1)*

The senior headquarters of a Communist task force has moved southward in the Laotian panhandle and some of its elements appear to have crossed into South Vietnam. *(Page 2)*

In Cambodia, the Communists continue to harass government positions along Routes 4 and 7. *(Page 3)*

A Soviet nuclear-powered submarine operated in the Caribbean for about a week late last month. *(Page 4)*

Bolivia

(Page 5)

50X1
50X1

Declassified in Part - Sanitized Copy Approved for Release 2016/06/14 : CIA-RDP79T00936A009100100001-5

JORDAN: Areas of Fighting

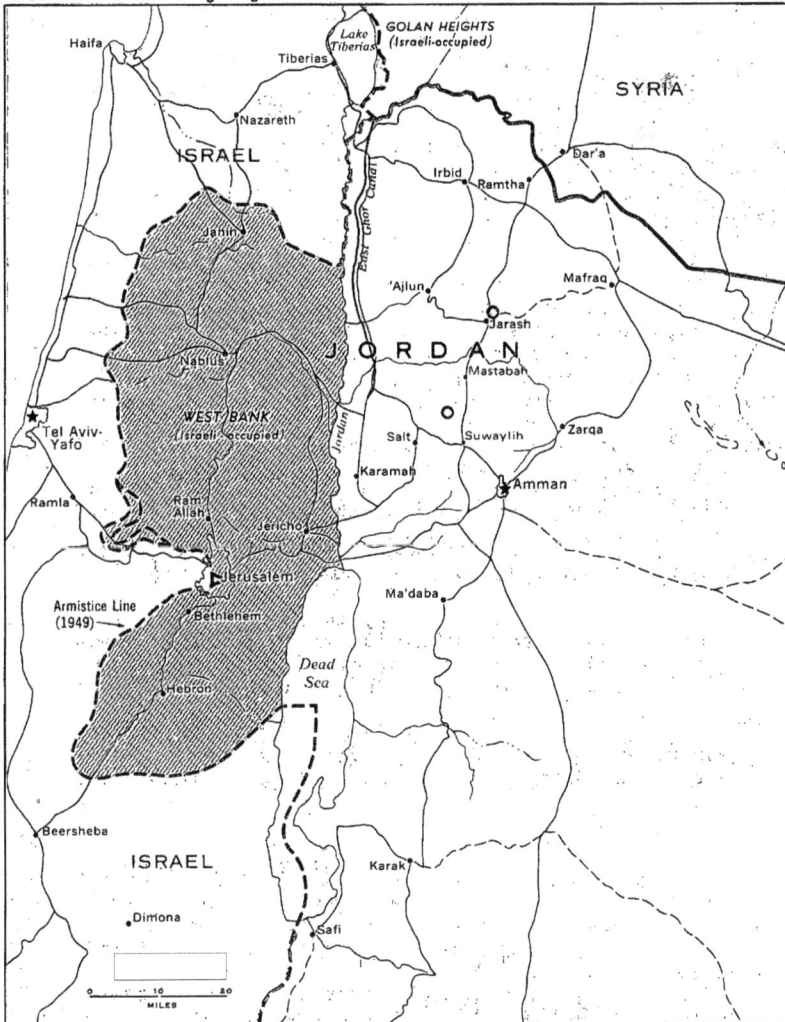

GOLAN HEIGHTS (Israeli-occupied)

Haifa

Lake Tiberias

Tiberias

SYRIA

Nazareth

ISRAEL

Irbid

Ramtha

Dar'a

Jahir

East Ghor Canal

'Ajlun

Mafraq

Jarash

Nablus

JORDAN

Mastabah

WEST BANK (Israeli occupied)

Jordan

Tel Aviv-Yafo

Salt

Suwaylih

Zarqa

Ramla

Karamah

Amman

Ram Allah

Jericho

Jerusalem

Bethlehem

Ma'daba

Armistice Line (1949)

Dead Sea

Hebron

Beersheba

ISRAEL

Karak

Dimona

Safi

10 20
MILES

50X1

550805 1-71 CIA

Declassified in Part - Sanitized Copy Approved for Release 2016/06/14 : CIA-RDP79T00936A009100100001-5

JORDAN

The army is maintaining heavy pressure on fedayeen centers in the hills northeast of Jarash and west of the Amman-Jarash road.

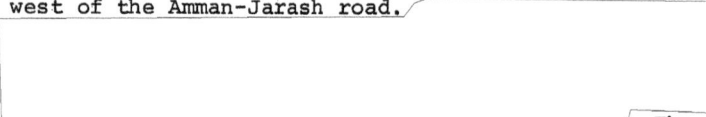

50X1

The village northeast of Amman where the fighting broke out on Friday appears to have been pacified.

> *Despite the continued fighting, the situation does not appear to be escalating to the scale of last September's civil war. The fedayeen seem too weak and disorganized to offer the resistance they showed then. The army probably is encouraged by the commandos' failure over the weekend to carry out more than sporadic firing in Amman, where the government is especially sensitive to guerrilla violence.*

50X1

50X1

50X1

1

Declassified in Part - Sanitized Copy Approved for Release 2016/06/14 : CIA-RDP79T00936A009100100001-5

Declassified in Part - Sanitized Copy Approved for Release 2016/06/14 : CIA-RDP79T00936A009100100001-5

NORTH
VIETNAM

Demilitarized Zone

Tchepone

QUANG TRI

THUA THIEN

Da Nang

QUANG NAM

LAOS

Elements of
infantry regiment

Senior
headquarters

QUANG TIN

2nd Division
headquarters

QUANG
NGAI

THAILAND

KONTUM

BINH
DINH

PLEIKU

PHU
BON

PHU
YEN

CAMBODIA

Tonle
Sap

DARLAC

KHANH
HOA

Mekong

QUANG
DUC

TUYEN

CAM
RANH

DUC

NINH
THUAN

PHUOC
LONG

BINH
LONG

LAM DONG

TAY
NINH

LONG
KHANH

BINH

BINH
DUONG

BINH
TUY

THUAN

BIEN
HOA

HAU
NGHIA

Saigon

SOUTH

KIEN
TUONG

CHINA

CHAU
DOC

KIEN
PHONG

LONG
AN

GIA
DINH

PHUOC
TUY

SEA

DINH
TUONG

GO
CONG

AN
GIANG

SA
DEC

VINH
LONG

KIEN HOA

KIEN
GIANG

PHONG
DINH

VINH
BINH

CHUONG
THIEN

BA XUYEN

GULF OF

SIAM

BAC LIEU

SOUTH VIETNAM

AN
XUYEN

50X1

0   100

MILES

550806 1-71 CIA

Declassified in Part - Sanitized Copy Approved for Release 2016/06/14 : CIA-RDP79T00936A009100100001-5

Declassified in Part - Sanitized Copy Approved for Release 2016/06/14 : CIA-RDP79T00936A009100100001-5

VIETNAM-LAOS

Recent intercepts show that the senior headquarters of a division-size Vietnamese Communist task force which had been in the Tchepone area of Laos last summer has moved farther south in the panhandle opposite South Vietnam's Quang Nam Province. Some of the combat elements under this headquarters, including at least part of an infantry regiment from the North Vietnamese 2nd Division and the division headquarters, appear already to have crossed into South Vietnam. The current locations of the remainder of the task force--including another regiment from the 2nd Division and an independent one-- are not known.

The southward shift of some elements of the 2nd Division back toward the South Vietnamese border was previously noted in The President's Daily Brief on 6 January. We expect that, during the next month or so, all of the units in the task force with which the 2nd Division is presently associated will move back to their former positions in Quang Nam, Quang Tin, and Quang Ngai provinces. Their return would roughly double Communist main force strength in this region.

Since the returning units presumably have been fleshed out and re-equipped, the Communists may soon be in a stronger position to challenge the government's progress in pacification along the populated eastern coastal area south of Da Nang.

2

Declassified in Part - Sanitized Copy Approved for Release 2016/06/14 : CIA-RDP79T00936A009100100001-5

Declassified in Part - Sanitized Copy Approved for Release 2016/06/14 : CIA-RDP79T00936A009100100001-5

CAMBODIA: Current Situation

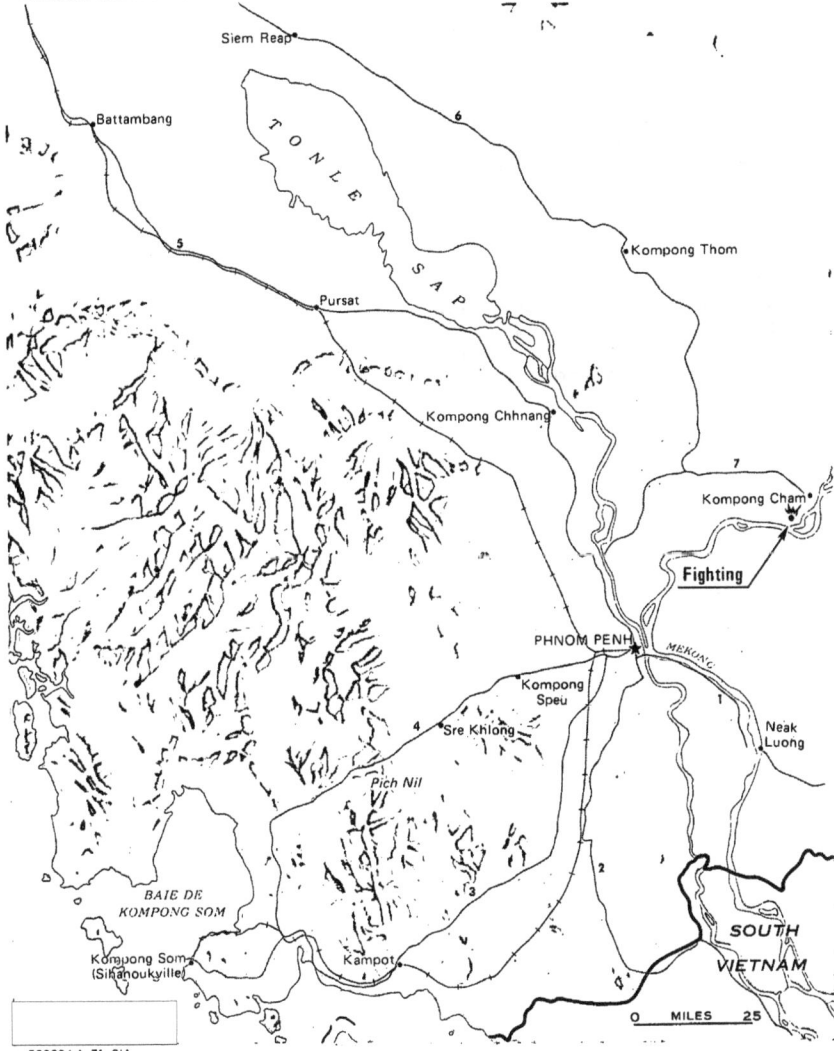

Siem Reap

Battambang

T O N L E

6

S A P

Kompong Thom

5

Pursat

Kompong Chhnang

7

Kompong Cham

Fighting

PHNOM PENH   MEKONG

Kompong
Speu

4   Sre Khlong

Neak
Luong

Pich Nil

BAIE DE
KOMPONG SOM

2

Kompong Som
(Sihanoukville)

Kampot

3

SOUTH
VIETNAM

0   MILES   25

50X1

550804 1-71 CIA

Declassified in Part - Sanitized Copy Approved for Release 2016/06/14 : CIA-RDP79T00936A009100100001-5

Declassified in Part - Sanitized Copy Approved for Release 2016/06/14 : CIA-RDP79T00936A009100100001-5

CAMBODIA

The Communists continue to harass government positions along Route 4 as government forces await orders to renew the drive to clear the Pich Nil pass. The South Vietnamese have begun putting supplies into Kompong Speu, but the clearing operation may not get under way until later this month. To the north, Communist harassment has increased along Route 7--which is still open--and some heavy fighting has broken out south of Kompong Cham city.

On the diplomatic front, Prime Minister Lon Nol plans to head a delegation to Saigon on 20 and 21 January. Discussions will cover both military and economic aspects of the South Vietnamese involvement in Cambodia, including Saigon's request that the Cambodians help pay the cost of South Vietnamese participation.

Earlier lower level negotiations foundered on the payments issue, and there is no evidence that either Lon Nol or Thieu is ready to compromise now. The two men met briefly in Cambodia several months ago. If Lon Nol goes ahead with the trip, it will be the first time he has left Cambodia since Sihanouk's ouster last March.

3

Declassified in Part - Sanitized Copy Approved for Release 2016/06/14 : CIA-RDP79T00936A009100100001-5

Declassified in Part - Sanitized Copy Approved for Release 2016/06/14 : CIA-RDP79T00936A009100100001-5

USSR-CUBA

A Soviet N-class nuclear-powered attack submarine operated in the Caribbean for about a week in late December,

50X1

> *This submarine, which was not previously detected in the area, is not known to have been serviced either in a Cuban port or by the Soviet tender then in the Caribbean. It could well have conducted ASW training with the guided-missile frigate which operated in the Caribbean for three days after leaving Cienfuegos on 23 December. The frigate and its supporting oiler entered the Baltic on 10 January.*

The tender and F-class diesel submarine which left the Caribbean on 3 January are in mid-Atlantic and still headed toward the Mediterranean. The Soviet rescue tug and the two nuclear submarine support barges remain in Cienfuegos.

4

Declassified in Part - Sanitized Copy Approved for Release 2016/06/14 : CIA-RDP79T00936A009100100001-5

Declassified in Part - Sanitized Copy Approved for Release 2016/06/14 : CIA-RDP79T00936A009100100001-5

NOTES

Bolivia: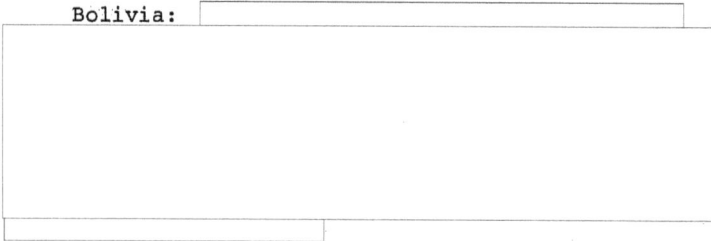

· 50X1
50X1

50X1

Uruguay: The government has still received no
demands from the kidnapers of British Ambassador
Jackson, but has publicly reaffirmed its policy of
no negotiation. Arrests made since the kidnaping
apparently have yielded no clue as to his where-
abouts. President Pacheco conferred Saturday with
his ministers of interior, defense, and foreign affairs at his vacation home on the northeast coast and
last night the government asked Congress to declare
a limited state of siege that would suspend some
personal rights.

5

Declassified in Part - Sanitized Copy Approved for Release 2016/06/14 : CIA-RDP79T00936A009100100001-5

Declassified in Part - Sanitized Copy Approved for Release 2016/06/14 : CIA-RDP79T00936A009100100001-5

Top Secret

Declassified in Part - Sanitized Copy Approved for Release 2016/06/14 : CIA-RDP79T00936A009100100001-5

Declassified in Part - Sanitized Copy Approved for Release 2016/06/14 : CIA-RDP79T00936A009100110001-4

The President's Daily Brief

12 January 1971

50

Top Secret

50X1

Declassified in Part - Sanitized Copy Approved for Release 2016/06/14 : CIA-RDP79T00936A009100110001-4

Declassified in Part - Sanitized Copy Approved for Release 2016/06/14 : CIA-RDP79T00936A009100110001-4

THE PRESIDENT'S DAILY BRIEF

12 January 1971

PRINCIPAL DEVELOPMENTS

The situation in Jordan is reported on *Page 1*.

50X1

In Bolivia, the government has moved quickly to put down a clumsy coup attempt and may be able to capitalize, at least for a time, on the episode. *(Page 2)*

Declassified in Part - Sanitized Copy Approved for Release 2016/06/14 : CIA-RDP79T00936A009100110001-4

JORDAN: Areas of Fighting

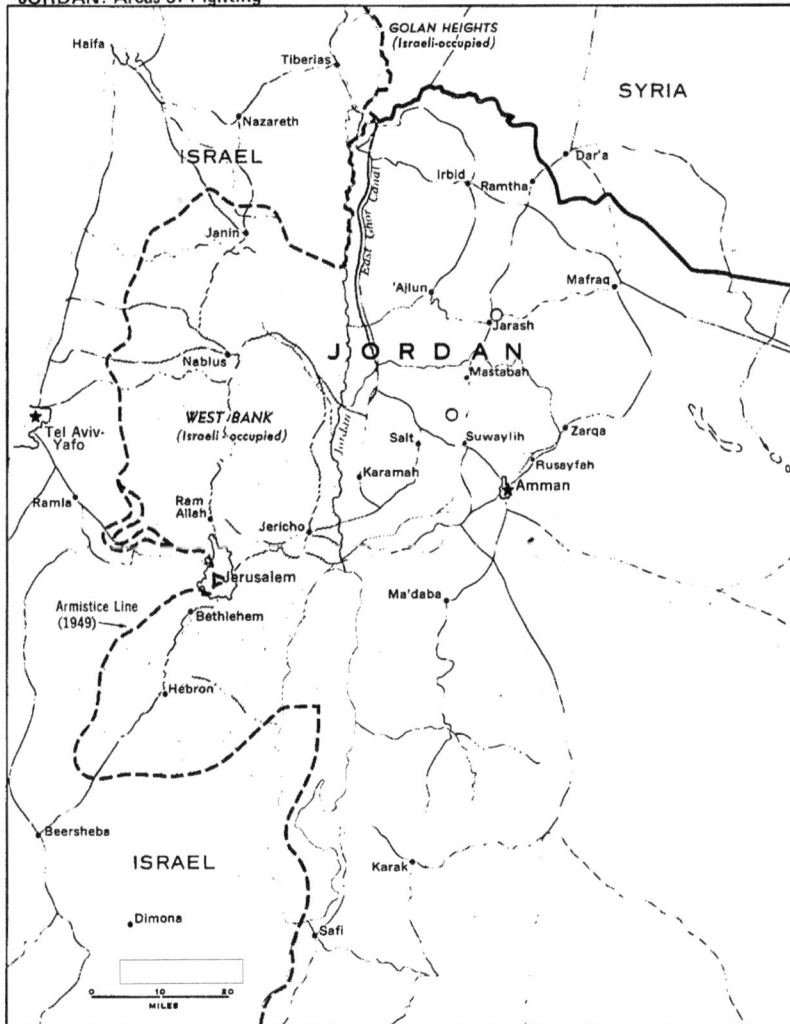

GOLAN HEIGHTS
(Israeli-occupied)

Haifa
Tiberias
SYRIA
Nazareth
ISRAEL
Irbid Ramtha Dar'a
Janin
'Ajlun Mafraq
Jarash
Nablus JORDAN Mastabah
WEST BANK
(Israeli occupied)
Tel Aviv-Yafo
Salt Suwaylih Zarqa
Karamah Rusayfah
Ramla Amman
Ram Allah
Jericho
Jerusalem
Ma'daba
Armistice Line
(1949) Bethlehem
Hebron
Beersheba
ISRAEL Karak
Dimona
Safi

10 20
MILES

550805 1-71 CIA

50X1

Declassified in Part - Sanitized Copy Approved for Release 2016/06/14 : CIA-RDP79T00936A009100110001-4

JORDAN

Fighting is continuing north of the capital on the outskirts of Jarash and to the west of the Amman-Jarash road, but the intensity has eased. In Amman, however, the situation remains tense. Small-arms fire persisted in the city throughout the day yesterday, keeping schools and businesses closed and the streets empty.

50X1

In addition, another group of commandos from the Saiqah organization sought and obtained army escort to the Syrian border.

> *These fedayeen actions are in contrast to the continuing stream of accusations being leveled against the government by Palestinian propagandists. In particular, they seem to belie Yasir Arafat's claim that the situation is "about to explode" because of the government's "liquidation plan" against the fedayeen.*

Premier Tal has invited cease-fire supervisor Ladgham to return to Jordan to assess the situation. Ladgham left Cairo this morning for London to meet with King Husayn, but is due to return to Egypt this evening. The Jordanian parliament is holding an emergency session this morning in anticipation of the scheduled meeting in Amman of delegations from the Arab states.

> *The Jordanian Government is generally maintaining a cool front even though it is concerned over the situation--especially over the future of Arab financial subsidies. The emphasis on patriotic fervor, emerging on special radio and TV programs, could be a clue that the army and the Crown Prince are prepared to press on with their tough policies despite Arab fulminations.*

1

Declassified in Part - Sanitized Copy Approved for Release 2016/06/14 : CIA-RDP79T00936A009100110001-4

Declassified in Part - Sanitized Copy Approved for Release 2016/06/14 : CIA-RDP79T00936A009100110001-4

NOTES

Bolivia: The half-baked attempt at a military coup in La Paz was put down handily yesterday, and there are no reports of disturbances in the country's interior. The attempt was apparently launched prematurely by dissatisfied officers who acted to avoid transfer to remote military posts. The neutralization of these military plotters should relieve some of the pressure that President Torres has been under during his three months in power. Labor and student groups supported Torres during this crisis, however, and their demands on the government for "revolutionary" action may rise several decibels.

USSR-Egypt:

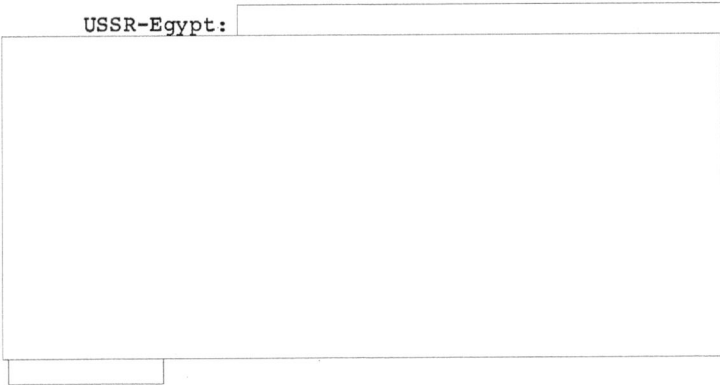

50X1)X1

50X1

2

Declassified in Part - Sanitized Copy Approved for Release 2016/06/14 : CIA-RDP79T00936A009100110001-4

Declassified in Part - Sanitized Copy Approved for Release 2016/06/14 : CIA-RDP79T00936A009100110001-4

Top Secret

Declassified in Part - Sanitized Copy Approved for Release 2016/06/14 : CIA-RDP79T00936A009100110001-4

Declassified in Part - Sanitized Copy Approved for Release 2016/06/14 : CIA-RDP79T00936A009100120001-3

The President's Daily Brief

13 January 1971

49

Top Secret 50X1

Declassified in Part - Sanitized Copy Approved for Release 2016/06/14 : CIA-RDP79T00936A009100120001-3

Declassified in Part - Sanitized Copy Approved for Release 2016/06/14 : CIA-RDP79T00936A009100120001-3

THE PRESIDENT'S DAILY BRIEF

13 January 1971

PRINCIPAL DEVELOPMENTS

The military situation in Cambodia is discussed on *Page 1*.

No progress was made yesterday toward a peaceful solution to the fighting in Jordan. *(Page 2)*

50X1

(Page 3)

50X1

The Soviets appear to be positioning three Y-class submarines for patrol duty in the western Atlantic. *(Page 4)*

The new Polish leadership seems anxious to establish a better rapport with East Germany. *(Page 5)*

Soviet progress in testing their new swing-wing bomber is noted on *Page 6*.

North Vietnam's infiltration starts have been low so far this month. *(Page 6)*

Declassified in Part - Sanitized Copy Approved for Release 2016/06/14 : CIA-RDP79T00936A009100120001-3

Declassified in Part - Sanitized Copy Approved for Release 2016/06/14 : CIA-RDP79T00936A009100120001-3

CAMBODIA: Current Situation

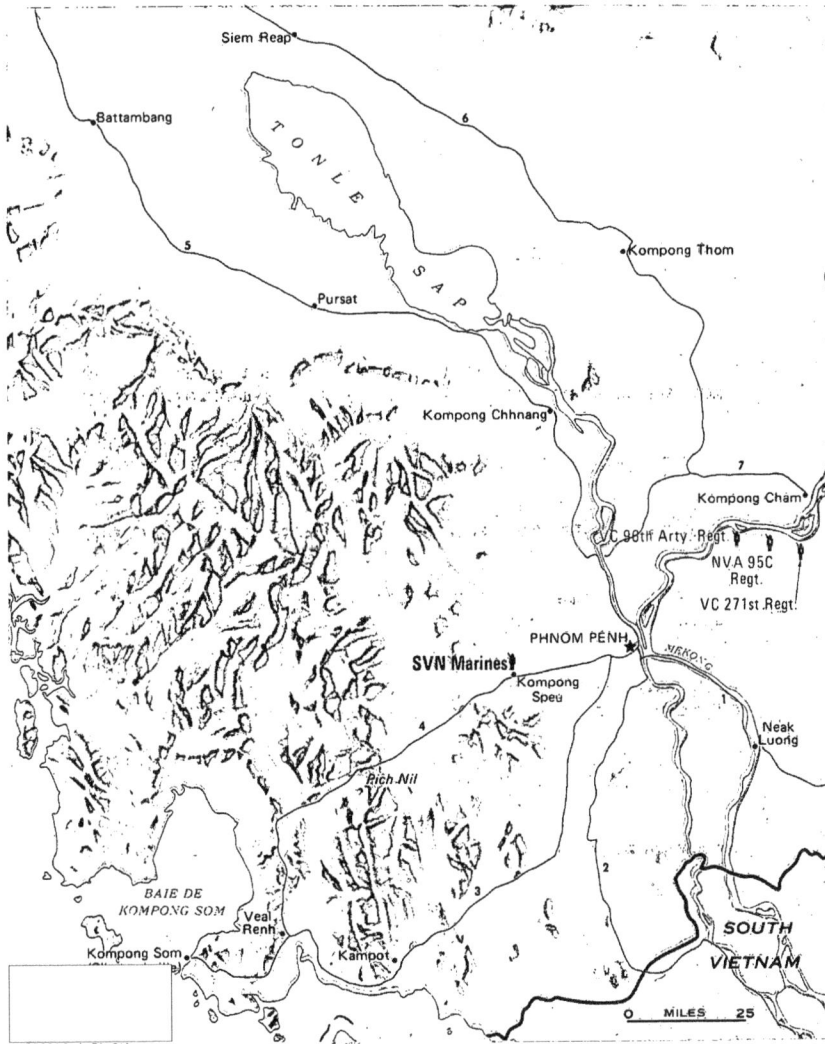

Siem Reap

Battambang

TONLE SAP

Kompong Thom

Pursat

Kompong Chhnang

Kompong Cham

VC 98th Arty Regt.

NVA 95C Regt.

VC 271st Regt.

PHNOM PENH

SVN Marines

Kompong Speu

Neak Luong

MEKONG

Pich Nil

BAIE DE KOMPONG SOM

Veal Renh

SOUTH VIETNAM

Kompong Som

Kampot

0   MILES   25

50X1

550815 1-71 CIA

Declassified in Part - Sanitized Copy Approved for Release 2016/06/14 : CIA-RDP79T00936A009100120001-3

Declassified in Part - Sanitized Copy Approved for Release 2016/06/14 : CIA-RDP79T00936A009100120001-3

CAMBODIA

Communications intelligence places the headquarters of the Viet Cong 96th Artillery Regiment on the south bank of the Mekong River, some 15 miles southwest of Kompong Cham city. This unit was last located in September 1970 when it was near the border of South Vietnam, 75 miles east of its current location.

> *The presence of the 96th Regiment increases the threat to Kompong Cham and to government forces operating along Route 7. The NVA 95C and VC 271st regiments are located near the 96th, but enemy activity in this area has been limited to scattered harassing attacks since the withdrawal of South Vietnamese troops from the Kompong Cham city environs late last month.*

Farther west, South Vietnamese forces are preparing for a clearing operation along Route 4. Three South Vietnamese marine battalions have arrived in Kompong Speu city, and ☐   50X1
☐ South Vietnamese rangers are also scheduled to   50X1
participate in the clearing operation. The rangers are to cross the border and move overland to Veal Renh in Kampot Province, where they will link up with Cambodian and Khmer Krom troops.

> *This route passes through Communist controlled territory, but the enemy may avoid a serious confrontation with South Vietnamese troops as they did in the Route 7 clearing operation.*

1

Declassified in Part - Sanitized Copy Approved for Release 2016/06/14 : CIA-RDP79T00936A009100120001-3

Declassified in Part - Sanitized Copy Approved for Release 2016/06/14 : CIA-RDP79T00936A009100120001-3

JORDAN

The situation in Jordan deteriorated further yesterday as indicated by the following events: the cease-fire concluded by government and fedayeen leaders did not take hold and the fighting that closed the city earlier in the day increased. Delegates from the various Arab states that helped negotiate the cease-fire last fall did not arrive in Amman as scheduled. Fedayeen propaganda became more brazen--a Fatah leader speaking in Damascus for example, called for the overthrow of King Husayn.

The best chances for a truce now lie with the moderating influence of cease-fire supervisor Ladgham, who met with Husayn yesterday in London. The army, meanwhile, is anxious to continue its militant campaign to bring the commandos under firm control, and this strategy apparently has the blessing of Jordan's leaders.

50X1

50X1

50X1

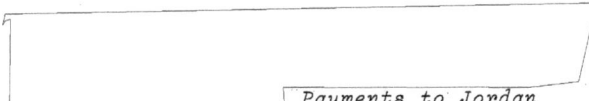

Payments to Jordan have been stopped by two of the three states that signed an agreement in Khartoum in 1967 to provide financial aid to states engaged in hostilities with Israel. Kuwait suspended its annual subsidy of $39 million early this month because of the renewed fighting between the Jordanian Army and the fedayeen, and Libya canceled its $25 million subsidy last September for the same reason. The third state, Saudi Arabia, is still making its annual payment of $41 million.

50X1

2

Declassified in Part - Sanitized Copy Approved for Release 2016/06/14 : CIA-RDP79T00936A009100120001-3

Declassified in Part - Sanitized Copy Approved for Release 2016/06/14 : CIA-RDP79T00936A009100120001-3

50X1

50X1

50X1

50X1

50X1

50X1

50X1

3

Declassified in Part - Sanitized Copy Approved for Release 2016/06/14 : CIA-RDP79T00936A009100120001-3

Declassified in Part - Sanitized Copy Approved for Release 2016/06/14 : CIA-RDP79T00936A009100120001-3

Y-class Submarine Patrols

Y-class

Y-class subs enroute to patrol stations

En route homeward

GREENLAND

50X1

Declassified in Part - Sanitized Copy Approved for Release 2016/06/14 : CIA-RDP79T00936A009100120001-3

Declassified in Part - Sanitized Copy Approved for Release 2016/06/14 : CIA-RDP79T00936A009100120001-3

USSR

A Y-class ballistic missile submarine currently in the Norwegian Sea and another now south of Iceland appear to be en route to patrol stations in the western Atlantic. A third Y-class is on station southeast of Bermuda. A fourth that had been on patrol northeast of Bermuda appears to be returning to the Northern Fleet.

> *Completion of these movements would mark the first time since June 1970 that the Soviets have had three Y-class submarines on simultaneous patrol in the western Atlantic. The Soviets have at least 14 operational Y-class units in the Northern Fleet, enough to support three Atlantic patrols on a continuing basis.*

4

Declassified in Part - Sanitized Copy Approved for Release 2016/06/14 : CIA-RDP79T00936A009100120001-3

Declassified in Part - Sanitized Copy Approved for Release 2016/06/14 : CIA-RDP79T00936A009100120001-3

POLAND

Members of the new Polish leadership have fanned out all over Eastern Europe this month to touch base with Poland's Warsaw Pact allies. The most important leaders--party leader Gierek and Prime Minister Jaroszewicz--visited Moscow and East Berlin. Their East German trip followed a three-day visit by Polish Foreign Minister Jedrychowski..

Although the new Polish leaders appear determined to establish their credentials throughout the Soviet orbit, they have given special precedence to East Germany. Relations between Ulbricht and Gomulka never were cordial, and Gierek appears anxious to ease the political and economic frictions that have developed between the two countries. Gierek has long been an advocate of closer industrial cooperation between East Germany and Poland, and he may use his ideas on this subject to promote a general improvement in bilateral relations.

5

Declassified in Part - Sanitized Copy Approved for Release 2016/06/14 : CIA-RDP79T00936A009100120001-3

New Soviet Swing-wing Bomber

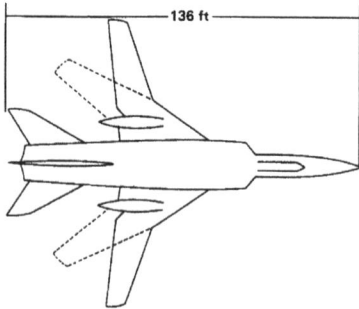

— 136 ft —

Combat radius ___ 2,900 nm with ASM, unrefueled
(at 460 kts)   3,900 nm with ASM, refueled
Max speed _____ 1,150 kts (Mach 2)
Year operational _____ 1974-76
Probably will carry one
air-to-surface missile

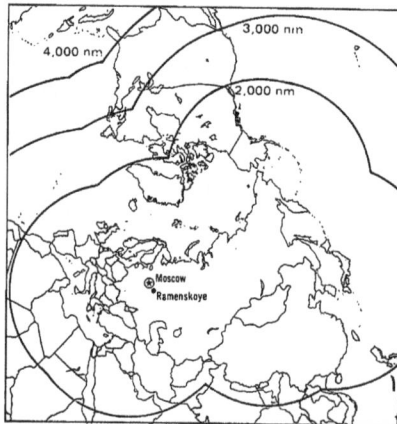

3,000 nm
4,000 nm
2,000 nm
Moscow
Ramenskoye

Prototypes at Ramenskoye flight test center

50X1·0X1

Declassified in Part - Sanitized Copy Approved for Release 2016/06/14 : CIA-RDP79T00936A009100120001-3

NOTES

USSR: Testing of the new swing-wing bomber--designated KAZ-A--evidently is proceeding rapidly and smoothly.

50X1

Although the KAZ-A appears best suited for operations against Europe and Asia, in-flight refueling would allow the aircraft to be used for two-way missions against the US, if it staged through bases in the Arctic.

North Vietnam: About 400 troops have been detected entering the infiltration system so far in January. The apparent drop in departures has occurred ⬚ disclosed North Vietnamese plans to dispatch one infiltration group, presumably battalion-sized, each night from 5 to 10 January. It is too early to determine if Hanoi has cut back on the troop flow. If there has been a slowdown, it may have been caused only by a North Vietnamese effort ⬚ -to shift the location of an important way station at the top of the infiltration system.

50X1

50X1
50X1

6

Declassified in Part - Sanitized Copy Approved for Release 2016/06/14 : CIA-RDP79T00936A009100120001-3

Declassified in Part - Sanitized Copy Approved for Release 2016/06/14 : CIA-RDP79T00936A009100120001-3

Top Secret

Declassified in Part - Sanitized Copy Approved for Release 2016/06/14 : CIA-RDP79T00936A009100120001-3

Declassified in Part - Sanitized Copy Approved for Release 2016/06/14 : CIA-RDP79T00936A009100130001-2

The President's Daily Brief

14 January 1971

50

Top Secret

50X1

Declassified in Part - Sanitized Copy Approved for Release 2016/06/14 : CIA-RDP79T00936A009100130001-2

Declassified in Part - Sanitized Copy Approved for Release 2016/06/14 : CIA-RDP79T00936A009100130001-2

THE PRESIDENT'S DAILY BRIEF

14 January 1971

PRINCIPAL DEVELOPMENTS

Egypt has made an informal proposal through the US
Interests Section in Cairo. *(Page 1)*

The situation in Jordan is discussed on *Page 2.*

50X1

(Page 3)   50X1

In Laos, the government has launched another harassing operation into the heart of the infiltration corridor. *(Page 4)*

In the aftermath of Monday's abortive coup, Torres
is encouraging leftist elements to expect radical
action by the government. *(Page 5)*

The breakdown in talks between Western oil companies
and petroleum exporting countries is discussed on
Page 6.

Week-long demonstrations in Manila are becoming in-
creasingly violent and are taking an anti-American
turn. *(Page 7)*

The joint South Vietnamese - Cambodian task forces
are moving toward the Pich Nil pass from north and
south. *(Page 8)*

Declassified in Part - Sanitized Copy Approved for Release 2016/06/14 : CIA-RDP79T00936A009100130001-2

Declassified in Part - Sanitized Copy Approved for Release 2016/06/14 : CIA-RDP79T00936A009100130001-2

EGYPT-ISRAEL

Retired General Abd al-Munim Amin, an original member of Nasir's Free Officers who claims close personal ties with President Sadat, has conveyed an "informal proposal" to the US Interests Section in Cairo in order to "achieve some progress toward peace before 5 February." The proposal, made on Sadat's behalf, allegedly grew out of Dayan's recent suggestion of mutual Israeli-Egyptian withdrawal to a limited distance from the Suez Canal. If the proposal received a positive response, Amin said, the Egyptians were willing to have it placed in official channels.

The plan conveyed by Amin calls for the Israelis to withdraw first to the Mitla hills, a natural line of defense some 40 kilometers east of the Canal. Egypt, for its part, would then "thin-out" its ground troops within a 40-kilometer zone west of the Canal but leave its air defense system in place. If these steps were taken, other measures could follow: work on opening the Canal to ship traffic, exchange of prisoners, abandonment of Cairo's threat to go to the Security Council, and the extension of talks through Jarring for another six months or a year. Cairo would also agree to proscribing flights of Egyptian and Israeli aircraft within an agreed distance from the Canal.

Amin said he would not be seeing Sadat again until 18 or 19 January when the President would be returning from the Aswan celebrations.

> *This approach comes at a curious time, as it cuts across the Jarring talks just as they are being launched again. More light on Egypt's motives may come if Minister Bergus has a follow-up meeting with Amin today as scheduled, but the proposal appears to underline again Egypt's anxiety to avoid expiration of the cease-fire. Cairo cannot expect a quick Israeli acceptance of this plan, but it may believe that if an exchange of views is in progress it will have a pretext to back off its February 5 ultimatum.*
>
> *Israel may find the proposal prickly to handle. Its content is clearly more forthcoming than the usual fare from Cairo. Moreover, Amin touted it as a response to Dayan's scheme and it is perhaps most significant as a signal that Egypt may be willing to get a dialogue--albeit informal-- going at last.*

1

Declassified in Part - Sanitized Copy Approved for Release 2016/06/14 : CIA-RDP79T00936A009100130001-2

Declassified in Part - Sanitized Copy Approved for Release 2016/06/14 : CIA-RDP79T00936A009100130001-2

JORDAN

The government and the central committee of the Palestine Liberation Organization reached another cease-fire agreement early this morning. The new pact, arranged in the presence of the Arab cease-fire observer commission, covers many of the same points listed in other agreements that have been made in the last four months. The most significant new point is that a joint government-fedayeen committee has defined locations for the fedayeen bases, and the fedayeen are required to go to these bases immediately.

> *The issue is whether the PLO central committee can carry out the new terms, for there is little doubt that the army will crack down quickly if there are violations of the cease-fire. The PLO leadership will be hard pressed to enforce the terms. The recent fighting has shown that it does not have the allegiance of the radical groups and that it has lost the loyalty of some members of Fatah and the Palestine Liberation Army.*

50X1

50X1

*   *   *

50X1

2

Declassified in Part - Sanitized Copy Approved for Release 2016/06/14 : CIA-RDP79T00936A009100130001-2

Declassified in Part - Sanitized Copy Approved for Release 2016/06/14 : CIA-RDP79T00936A009100130001-2

50X1

50X1

Declassified in Part - Sanitized Copy Approved for Release 2016/06/14 : CIA-RDP79T00936A009100130001-2

Declassified in Part - Sanitized Copy Approved for Release 2016/06/14 : CIA-RDP79T00936A009100130001-2

SOUTHERN YEMEN

50X1

50X1

50X1

50X1

50X1

50X1

3

Declassified in Part - Sanitized Copy Approved for Release 2016/06/14 : CIA-RDP79T00936A009100130001-2

Declassified in Part - Sanitized Copy Approved for Release 2016/06/14 : CIA-RDP79T00936A009100130001-2

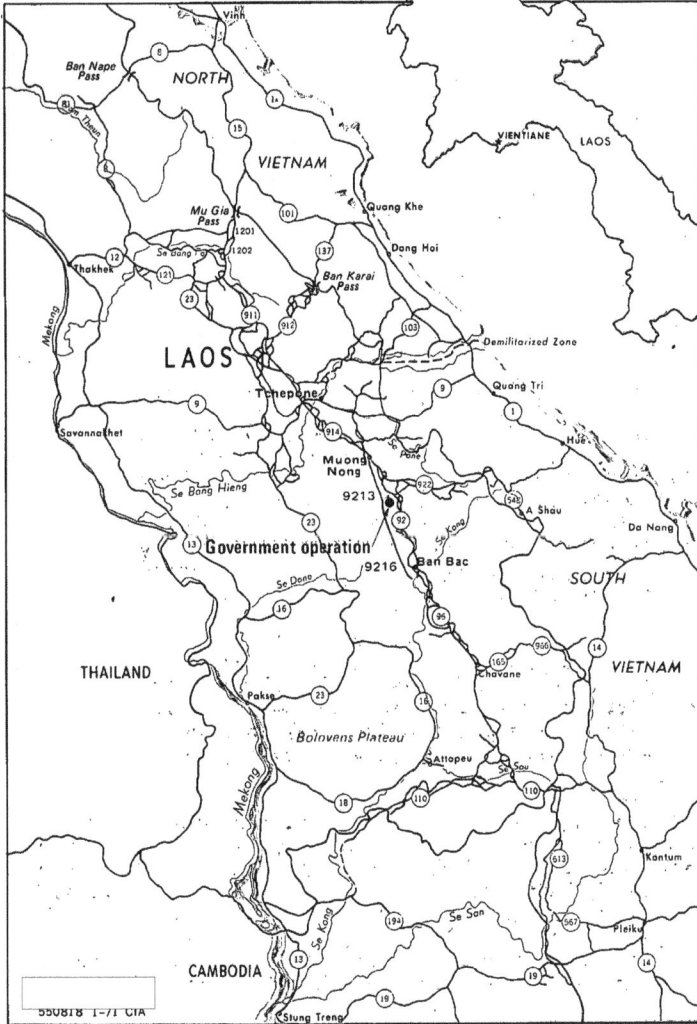

LAOS: Government operation launched

50X1

Declassified in Part - Sanitized Copy Approved for Release 2016/06/14 : CIA-RDP79T00936A009100130001-2

Declassified in Part - Sanitized Copy Approved for Release 2016/06/14 : CIA-RDP79T00936A009100130001-2

LAOS

Four government irregular battalions plus three special action teams and an intelligence team have been airlifted to eastern Savannakhet Province in an attempt to interdict Route 9213, the road recently completed by the Communists as an alternative to heavily bombed routes 92 and 96. The units also hope to destroy enemy supply depots and installations in the area.

> *Although the government forces have encountered no resistance thus far, the Communists are likely to want to contest this latest operation. No major Communist combat units are known to be in the immediate area, however, and a significant counterattack may be slow to develop.*
>
> *This is the third government operation into the infiltration corridor this dry season. One earlier effort managed to get into the Communist supply center at Tchepone for three days, while a second, into the Ban Bac area, ran into heavy opposition in its attempt to harass Route 96.*

4

Declassified in Part - Sanitized Copy Approved for Release 2016/06/14 : CIA-RDP79T00936A009100130001-2

Declassified in Part - Sanitized Copy Approved for Release 2016/06/14 : CIA-RDP79T00936A009100130001-2

BOLIVIA

Addressing a large "antifascist" rally in La Paz on Tuesday, President Torres said he would begin immediate discussions with students, workers, and representatives of popular organizations to form a "popular assembly." Repeating previous promises that additional unspecified "revolutionary measures" would be taken, he said he would extend the revolution "to the limits the people desire." He added that the activities of "some international agencies" (a common expression in La Paz for the US Government) were being investigated. The national labor organization is already calling for expulsion of all "imperialist missions."

Torres has begun paying his debt to the leftist groups that opposed Monday's abortive coup. By encouraging leftist elements to expect immediate radical action, however, Torres is fostering the growth of pressure on the government to satisfy the varying demands.

50X1

50X1

50X1

50X1

50X1

5

Declassified in Part - Sanitized Copy Approved for Release 2016/06/14 : CIA-RDP79T00936A009100130001-2

Declassified in Part - Sanitized Copy Approved for Release 2016/06/14 : CIA-RDP79T00936A009100130001-2

INTERNATIONAL OIL

The Organization of Petroleum Exporting Countries (OPEC) is to meet in emergency session Tuesday to work out its next move following the break-off of talks with Western oil companies in Tehran. Negotiations between the companies and the OPEC subcommittee collapsed on 12 January when OPEC refused to deal with the low-level officials sent by the companies.

50X1

50X1

50X1

The Shah is irate that the Consortium was unprepared to negotiate with the subcommittee this week, but two Iranian Government officials have been more conciliatory. They say that negotiations could still be held if top-level Consortium negotiators were to arrive in Tehran quickly.

OPEC, with headquarters in Vienna, embraces Iran, Libya, Saudi Arabia, Kuwait, Iraq, Abu Dhabi, Qatar, Indonesia, Algeria, and Venezuela. The present agreement on oil negotiations is one of the few times radical and moderate members of the group have joined together even temporarily to present a united front to the oil companies.

6

Declassified in Part - Sanitized Copy Approved for Release 2016/06/14 : CIA-RDP79T00936A009100130001-2

Declassified in Part - Sanitized Copy Approved for Release 2016/06/14 : CIA-RDP79T00936A009100130001-2

PHILIPPINES

A strike by drivers of Manila's jeepneys—mini-buses that are a major part of the city's transportation system—has brought near paralysis to the city. The strike, sparked by a hike in gasoline prices, is supported by student activists critical of the American oil companies involved in the price rise. Several youths were fatally shot yesterday by Manila police who were attempting to disperse the demonstrators.

> *These deaths are likely to inflate an already ugly mood, and demonstrations at the US Embassy could develop. The student radicals, after a summer and fall of relative inactivity, now have found a cause—one that can be linked with the anniversary on 26 January of last year's student violence.*

50X1

50X1

50X1

50X1

7

Declassified in Part - Sanitized Copy Approved for Release 2016/06/14 : CIA-RDP79T00936A009100130001-2

Declassified in Part - Sanitized Copy Approved for Release 2016/06/14 : CIA-RDP79T00936A009100130001-2

CAMBODIA: Current Situation

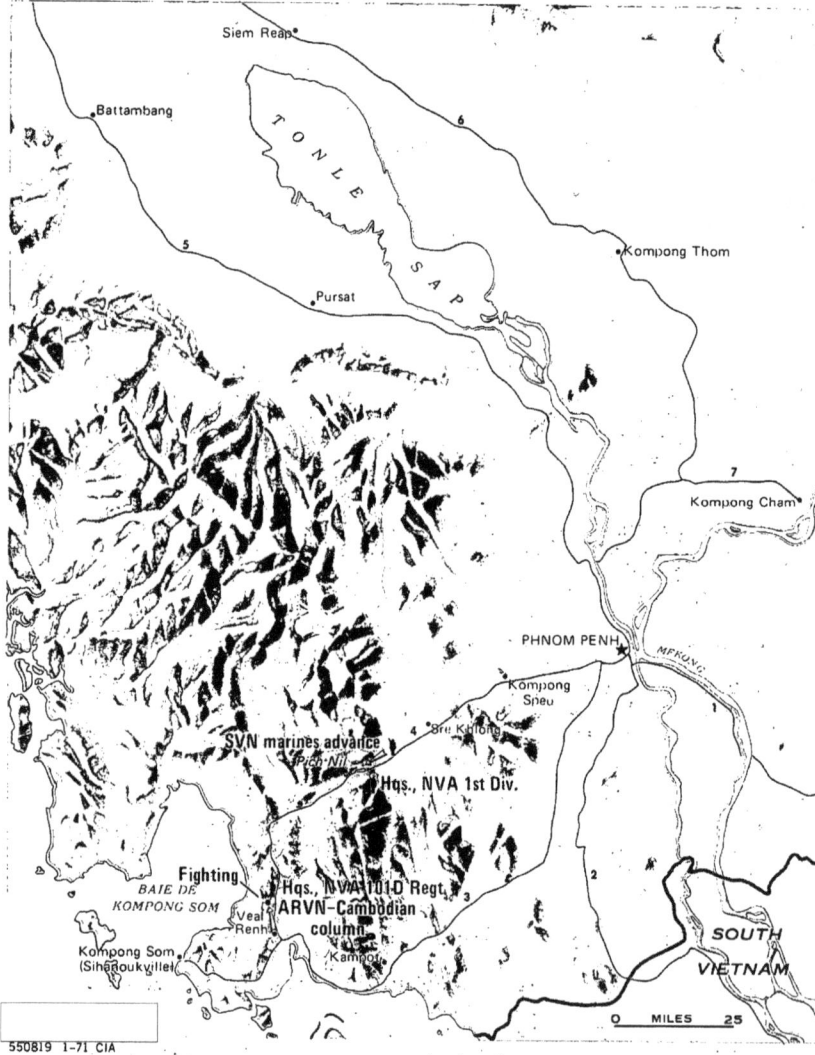

Siem Reap

Battambang

TONLE SAP

6

5

Kompong Thom

Pursat

7

Kompong Cham

PHNOM PENH

MEKONG

Kompong Speu

1

SVN marines advance
Pich Nil

Bru Khlong

Hqs., NVA 1st Div.

Fighting
BAIE DE
KOMPONG SOM

Hqs., NVA 101D Regt,
ARVN-Cambodian
column

2

3

Veal
Renh

Kampot

Kompong Som
(Sihanoukville)

SOUTH
VIETNAM

0 MILES 25

550819 1-71 CIA

50X1

Declassified in Part - Sanitized Copy Approved for Release 2016/06/14 : CIA-RDP79T00936A009100130001-2

Declassified in Part - Sanitized Copy Approved for Release 2016/06/14 : CIA-RDP79T00936A009100130001-2

NOTE

Cambodia: South Vietnamese lead elements of the task force pushing up from the south along Route 4 claimed they killed 30 Communists in their first skirmish with the enemy yesterday a few miles north of Veal Renh. Some of the enemy casualties may have been from the North Vietnamese 101D Regiment, whose headquarters recently was located 15 miles north of Veal Renh. Press reports indicate that South Vietnamese marine units with the smaller task force coming from the north had moved to within five miles of Pich Nil pass early yesterday. Intercepts placed the NVA 1st Division in the vicinity of Pich Nil on 8 January, but if the Communists follow past tactics they will try to avoid major fighting.

8

Declassified in Part - Sanitized Copy Approved for Release 2016/06/14 : CIA-RDP79T00936A009100130001-2

Declassified in Part - Sanitized Copy Approved for Release 2016/06/14 : CIA-RDP79T00936A009100130001-2

Top Secret

Declassified in Part - Sanitized Copy Approved for Release 2016/06/14 : CIA-RDP79T00936A009100130001-2

Declassified in Part - Sanitized Copy Approved for Release 2016/06/14 : CIA-RDP79T00936A009100140001-1

The President's Daily Brief

15 January 1971

48

Top Secret 50X1

Declassified in Part - Sanitized Copy Approved for Release 2016/06/14 : CIA-RDP79T00936A009100140001-1

Declassified in Part - Sanitized Copy Approved for Release 2016/06/14 : CIA-RDP79T00936A009100140001-1

THE PRESIDENT'S DAILY BRIEF

15 January 1971

PRINCIPAL DEVELOPMENTS

On *Page 1* South Vietnam's   50X1

The Pathet Lao   50X1
designed to revive the possibility of   50X1
peace talks.   *(Page 2)*

The Soviets have diluted a pre-Christmas offer on
Berlin access. *(Page 4)*

In the Dominican Republic, a successful police raid
has at least temporarily crippled the leadership of
the organization primarily responsible for terrorism
in recent years. *(Page 6)*

On *Page 7* we appraise Jordanian reports of Iraqi
troop withdrawals from Jordan.

Yesterday morning's cease-fire agreement in Jordan
was effective during its first day. *(Page 8)*

Declassified in Part - Sanitized Copy Approved for Release 2016/06/14 : CIA-RDP79T00936A009100140001-1

Declassified in Part - Sanitized Copy Approved for Release 2016/06/14 : CIA-RDP79T00936A009100140001-1

Map of South Vietnam showing Military Regions (MR 1, MR 2, MR 3, MR 4), provinces, and neighboring countries.

Labels visible on map:

NORTH VIETNAM

Demilitarized Zone

Savannakhet

Quang Tri
QUANG TRI
Hue
THUA THIEN
A Shau
Da Nang
MR 1

Saravane

LAOS

QUANG NAM

THAILAND
Warin Chamrap
Pakse

QUANG TIN

QUANG NGAI   Quang Ngai

KONTUM

Kontum

BINH DINH

Pleiku
PLEIKU

Qui Nhon

PHU BON
PHU YEN
MR 2

CAMBODIA

DARLAC

Ban Me Thuot

KHANH HOA
Nha Trang

Tonle Sap

Mekong

QUANG DUC

TUYEN DUC   Da Lat

NINH THUAN

CAM RANH

PHUOC LONG
Loc Ninh
BINH LONG

PHNOM PENH

LAM DONG

TAY NINH
Tay Ninh

BINH DUONG

LONG KHANH

BINH THUAN

SOUTH CHINA SEA

BIEN HOA

MAU NGHIA
KIEN TUONG
KIEN PHONG
CHAU DOC

SAIGON
LONG AN
GO CONG
PHUOC TUY
MR 3
Vung Tau

AN GIANG
SA DEC
DINH TUONG
MY THO
KIEN HOA

Capital Special Zone

KIEN GIANG
Can Tho
PHONG DINH
VINH LONG
VINH BINH

GULF OF SIAM

CHUONG THIEN

BA XUYEN

Ca Mau
BAC LIEU
MR 4

AN XUYEN

SOUTH VIETNAM

0   100
MILES

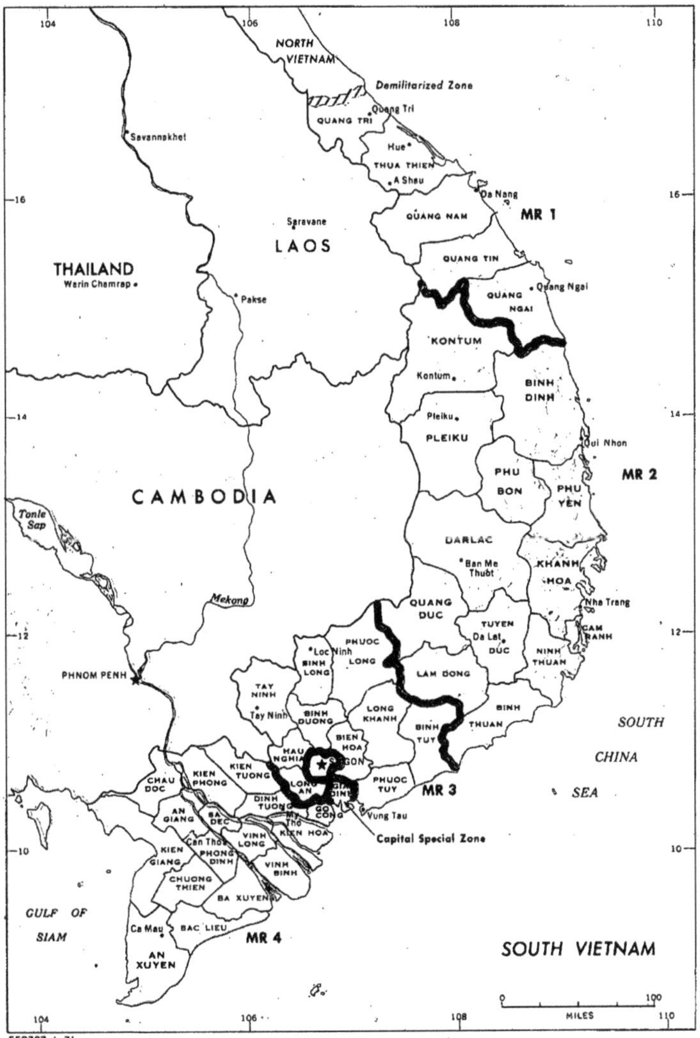

550787 1-71

Declassified in Part - Sanitized Copy Approved for Release 2016/06/14 : CIA-RDP79T00936A009100140001-1

Declassified in Part - Sanitized Copy Approved for Release 2016/06/14 : CIA-RDP79T00936A009100140001-1

SOUTH VIETNAM

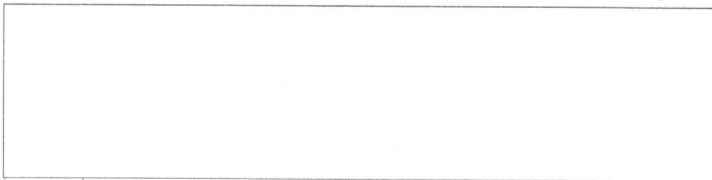 50X1

50X1
50X1

50X1
50X1

50X1
50X1

50X1

1

Declassified in Part - Sanitized Copy Approved for Release 2016/06/14 : CIA-RDP79T00936A009100140001-1

Declassified in Part - Sanitized Copy Approved for Release 2016/06/14 : CIA-RDP79T00936A009100140001-1

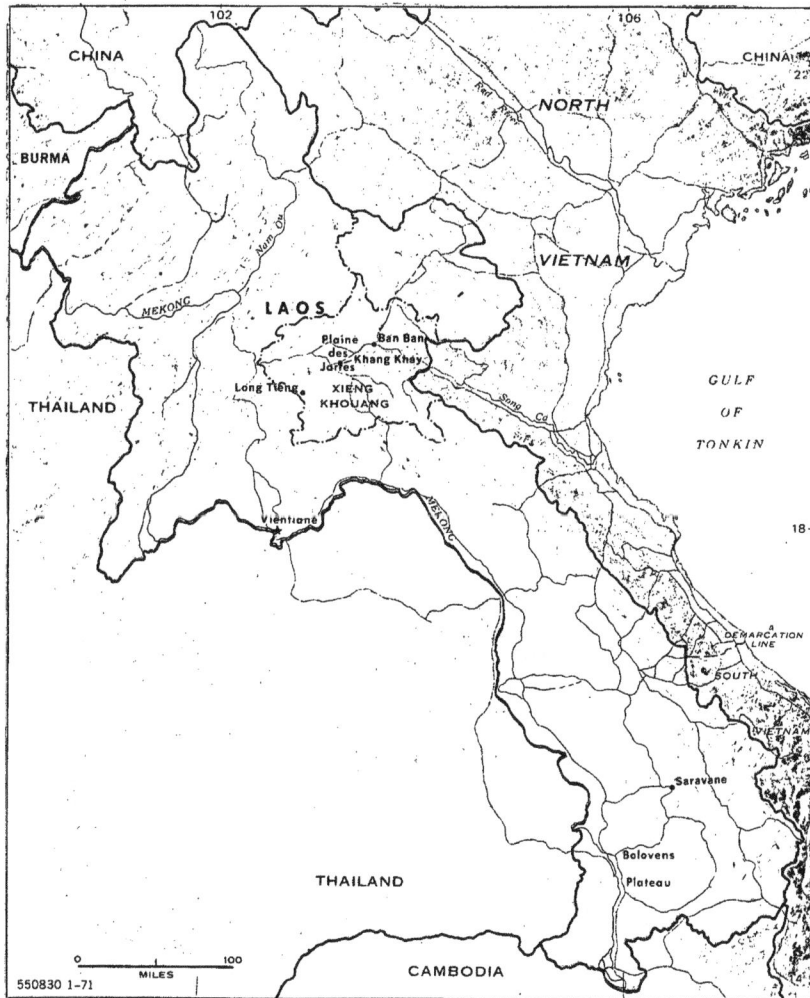

Declassified in Part - Sanitized Copy Approved for Release 2016/06/14 : CIA-RDP79T00936A009100140001-1

Declassified in Part - Sanitized Copy Approved for Release 2016/06/14 : CIA-RDP79T00936A009100140001-1

LAOS

The Pathet Lao representative in Vientiane, Soth Phetrasy, recently commented [   ] that the US would have to weigh in with Souvanna, who was taking an "intransigent stand," if there were to be any further progress toward Lao peace talks. According to Soth, the Pathet Lao understood the concern in both Vientiane and Washington that a bombing halt in Xieng Khouang Province, as proposed by the Communists as part of the security precautions for talks in Khang Khay, would jeopardize the headquarters of the irregulars at Long Tieng. He argued, however, that the bombing could be resumed any time Souvanna felt that the negotiations were getting nowhere.

50X1
50X1

Soth's comment about Souvanna's intransigence is a reference to the last Pathet Lao meeting with the Prime Minister on 31 December. At that session the Communists dropped their insistence that the bombing halt also apply to Samneua Province, but failed to evoke any counteroffer from Souvanna.

[   ] appear to be part of a fresh Communist effort to revive the possibility of talks at Khang Khay. Both Soth and the Pathet Lao special negotiator have recently been complaining of Souvanna's adamant stand to various Lao officials in Vientiane, possibly as much in the hope of convincing Souvanna's rightist critics that there is something to be gained by negotiations as in the hope of driving them further from Souvanna.

50X1

It is possible that the Communists are now merely going through the motions of trying to get talks under way in order to justify a forthcoming campaign against Vang Pao's irregulars. A unilateral bombing halt in Xieng Khouang would, of course, be a boon to the Communists if their aim is to move additional forces--such as the North Vietnamese 312th Division--onto the Plaine des Jarres uncontested and to position supplies for a major drive against Long Tieng.

(continued)

2

Declassified in Part - Sanitized Copy Approved for Release 2016/06/14 : CIA-RDP79T00936A009100140001-1

Declassified in Part - Sanitized Copy Approved for Release 2016/06/14 : CIA-RDP79T00936A009100140001-1

*It is doubtful that the Communists believe
Souvanna would stop the bombing without
some concessions on their part, such as
agreeing not to introduce new troops into
Xieng Khouang or accepting a local cease-
fire. This would give Vang Pao's forces
a respite during a time when the Communists
are usually taking advantage of good weather
for offensive operations. Whether the Communists are prepared to discuss such steps
is not clear, however, in part because Souvanna has not yet explored the possibilities.*

3

Declassified in Part - Sanitized Copy Approved for Release 2016/06/14 : CIA-RDP79T00936A009100140001-1

Declassified in Part - Sanitized Copy Approved for Release 2016/06/14 : CIA-RDP79T00936A009100140001-1

USSR - BERLIN - WEST GERMANY

At a four-power advisers' meeting on 13 January, the Soviets diluted an offer on access which they had advanced before the holidays. Soviet Ambassador Abrasimov had suggested on 19 December that East Germany might be willing to guarantee "sealed cargo transport" between West Germany and Berlin and to eliminate "certain freight documents." In the latest meeting, the Soviets insisted that East German officials would retain the right to inspect cargoes before sealing and that only insignificant changes in the handling of documents were possible.

> *The Soviets offered nothing to advance the pace of negotiations; their remarks suggest that they have little immediate interest in negotiating on access arrangements in a four-power context. Although they proposed that drafting begin on the language of a four-power statement on principles, they showed no inclination to offer any concessions on substance. They continued to rehash other standard positions such as the limitations to be placed on the West German presence in Berlin.*
>
> *These tactics may reflect an assessment that Allied opposition to access talks between Bonn and Pankow can be overcome. The Soviets presumably would not wish to prejudice the East German negotiating position in advance, if there were a possibility that bilateral talks on access would get under way in the near future.*

50X1

(continued)

4

Declassified in Part - Sanitized Copy Approved for Release 2016/06/14 : CIA-RDP79T00936A009100140001-1

Declassified in Part - Sanitized Copy Approved for Release 2016/06/14 : CIA-RDP79T00936A009100140001-1

50X1

5

Declassified in Part - Sanitized Copy Approved for Release 2016/06/14 : CIA-RDP79T00936A009100140001-1

Declassified in Part - Sanitized Copy Approved for Release 2016/06/14 : CIA-RDP79T00936A009100140001-1

DOMINICAN REPUBLIC

On Wednesday Dominican police arrested six leaders of the extremist Dominican Revolutionary Movement (MPD). The US Embassy in Santo Domingo notes that the MPD national leadership has been at least temporarily crippled.

50X1

50X1

50X1

50X1

6

Declassified in Part - Sanitized Copy Approved for Release 2016/06/14 : CIA-RDP79T00936A009100140001-1

Declassified in Part - Sanitized Copy Approved for Release 2016/06/14 : CIA-RDP79T00936A009100140001-1

IRAQ-JORDAN

Jordanian Prime Minister Tal told Ambassador Brown Wednesday that the Iraqis were steadily withdrawing their troops from Jordan, and that he believed they were heading for total evacuation. Tal said he expected to take over the Mafraq area in about a week.

Jordanian officials have been making similarly optimistic statements for some time. Although Iraqi troops have been reduced from about 25,000 last fall to somewhat less than 10,000 now--the lowest level since they arrived in June 1967--the force in Jordan is still substantial. The test of the Iraqis' intentions will be whether they in fact leave their main base at Mafraq.

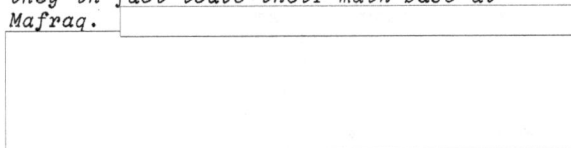

50X1
50X1

A decision by Baghdad to withdraw most of its forces would be based on fear that the Jordanian Army might move against the troops, on concern over the soldiers' low morale, and on renewed apprehension over rising Kurdish dissident activity in northern Iraq. Even if Tal's optimism is generally warranted, Baghdad may leave at least a token force in Jordan if only to maintain its anti-Israeli credentials in Arab councils.

7

Declassified in Part - Sanitized Copy Approved for Release 2016/06/14 : CIA-RDP79T00936A009100140001-1

Declassified in Part - Sanitized Copy Approved for Release 2016/06/14 : CIA-RDP79T00936A009100140001-1

NOTES

Jordan: The army and the fedayeen have started to carry out the provisions of the cease-fire agreement reached yesterday morning, and Amman began returning to normal during the day. Premier Tal is in an ebullient mood over achieving the agreement despite the efforts of the Egyptian cease-fire observer to water down some sections the commandos had accepted.

50X1

Many army elements similarly dismiss the agreement as only a temporary "piece of paper."

Chile: The Bethlehem Steel Company has been given until 1 February to conclude a contract for sale of its iron mine and related assets in Chile on government terms. On that date the government steel company will begin direct supervision of all Bethlehem operations. Payment for the assets, whose value will be determined by the government, will be made in ore or money at Chile's option and will extend over 30 years at three percent interest. Bethlehem officials, who had hoped to operate normally under the Allende administration, have termed the Chilean plan "confiscatory."

USSR-Cuba:

50X1

the Soviet N-class submarine previously thought to have operated in the Caribbean late last month (reported in The President's Daily Brief of 11 January) was southeast of Bermuda at that time and probably did not operate in the Caribbean.

8

Declassified in Part - Sanitized Copy Approved for Release 2016/06/14 : CIA-RDP79T00936A009100140001-1

Declassified in Part - Sanitized Copy Approved for Release 2016/06/14 : CIA-RDP79T00936A009100140001-1

Top Secret

Declassified in Part - Sanitized Copy Approved for Release 2016/06/14 : CIA-RDP79T00936A009100140001-1

Declassified in Part - Sanitized Copy Approved for Release 2016/06/14 : CIA-RDP79T00936A009100160001-9

The President's Daily Brief

18 January 1971

49

Top Secret

50X1

Declassified in Part - Sanitized Copy Approved for Release 2016/06/14 : CIA-RDP79T00936A009100160001-9

Declassified in Part - Sanitized Copy Approved for Release 2016/06/14 : CIA-RDP79T00936A0091100160001-9

THE PRESIDENT'S DAILY BRIEF

18 January 1971

PRINCIPAL DEVELOPMENTS

The Egyptian letter to Jarring is discussed on *Page 1*.

East and West Germany.   50X1

(Page 2)   50X1

Another enemy regiment has moved from Cambodia into Tay Ninh Province. *(Page 3)*

The situation in Cambodia is noted on *Page 4*.

Laotian irregulars are meeting increased resistance in their operation against the new road in the infiltration corridor. *(Page 5)*

Declassified in Part - Sanitized Copy Approved for Release 2016/06/14 : CIA-RDP79T00936A0091100160001-9

Declassified in Part - Sanitized Copy Approved for Release 2016/06/14 : CIA-RDP79T00936A009100160001-9

MIDDLE EAST

The Egyptian letter presented to Jarring on 15 January charges that Israel's proposal "adds no new element" to previous Israeli positions and that it ignores the question of Israeli withdrawal from occupied territories and the refugee problem. The letter calls for an end to "Israeli aggression," the withdrawal of all Israeli forces to their 5 June 1967 positions and a settlement of the refugee problem through Israeli respect for the rights of the Palestinian people in accordance with UN resolutions. The letter says that the Security Council could provide security to all states in the area by setting up a UN peace-keeping force composed of the Big Four powers and by establishing demilitarized zones astride the borders.

The letter concludes by stating that the Security Council "must exercise its responsibility for international peace and security" because the Israeli position impedes the achievement of a peaceful settlement and leads to continued escalation in the Middle East.

Jarring told Ambassador Yost that he is recasting the Egyptian letter in order to eliminate its "polemical" elements and to put it in a form resembling the Israelis' proposals. He plans to show this to Egyptian Ambassador Zayyat today and hopes to get his concurrence to the new draft without reference to Cairo.

> It seems doubtful that Zayyat will accede to any major revisions without consulting Cairo. At any rate, even stripped of its polemics, Cairo's letter is uncompromising on Israeli withdrawal and the refugee question. The areas of disagreement seem as wide as ever.

> It is unclear from the letter whether Cairo is calling for another Security Council meeting. Zayyat says he is seeking clarification from Cairo on the point but he told Ambassador Yost that his personal interpretation was that the language was intended neither to request a Security Council meeting nor to foreclose this option. In Cairo, the Egyptian Foreign Ministry summoned separately yesterday the ambassadors of non-permanent members of the Security Council, presumably to discuss what action the Council might take.

1

Declassified in Part - Sanitized Copy Approved for Release 2016/06/14 : CIA-RDP79T00936A009100160001-9

Declassified in Part - Sanitized Copy Approved for Release 2016/06/14 : CIA-RDP79T00936A0091001600001-9

EAST GERMANY - WEST GERMANY

50X1

50X1
50X1

50X1

50X1

50X1

2

Declassified in Part - Sanitized Copy Approved for Release 2016/06/14 : CIA-RDP79T00936A0091001600001-9

Declassified in Part - Sanitized Copy Approved for Release 2016/06/14 : CIA-RDP79T00936A009100160001-9

Recent Communist Unit Relocation

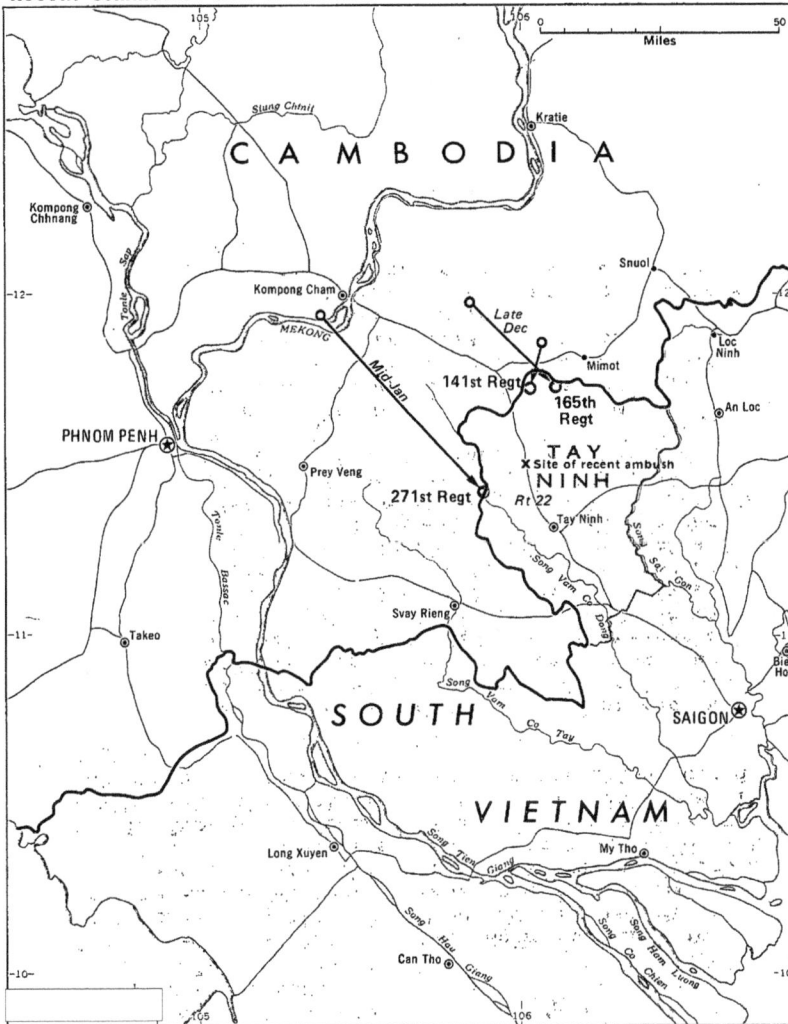

50X1

550836 1-71 CIA

Declassified in Part - Sanitized Copy Approved for Release 2016/06/14 : CIA-RDP79T00936A009100160001-9

Declassified in Part - Sanitized Copy Approved for Release 2016/06/14 : CIA-RDP79T00936A009100160001-9

SOUTH VIETNAM - CAMBODIA

The 271st Regiment of the Communist 9th Division, which participated in the campaign in the Kompong Cham area several weeks ago, has moved more than 40 miles to the southeast into the Tay Ninh Province border area of South Vietnam. Two enemy soldiers, who had taken part in an ambush of a South Vietnamese supply convoy on Route 22, claim that parts of the regiment returned to Tay Ninh during the first two weeks of January.

50X1

Two regiments of the Communist 7th Division--the 141st and 165th--which moved into northern Tay Ninh Province late last month appear ready for action.

50X1

The continuing movement of forces to northern Tay Ninh appears intended to discourage South Vietnamese operations into Cambodia. The two regiments of the 7th Division, as well as the 271st Regiment, are close to Route 22, and they may coordinate harassing action against this major supply route into Cambodia.

Declassified in Part - Sanitized Copy Approved for Release 2016/06/14 : CIA-RDP79T00936A009100160001-9

Declassified in Part - Sanitized Copy Approved for Release 2016/06/14 : CIA-RDP79T00936A009100160001-9

CAMBODIA: Current Situation

Siem Reap

Battambang

T O N L E

S A P

Kompong Thom

Pursat

Kompong Chhnang

Kompong Cham

PHNOM PENH

MEKONG

Neak Luong

Cambodians advance
Pich Nil

S. Vietnamese advance

Stung Chhay

Hqs. NVA 101D Regt.

BAIE DE KOMPONG SOM

Veal Renh

Kompong Som
(Sihanoukville)

Kampot

SOUTH

VIETNAM

50X1

550837 1-71 CIA

0   MILES   25

Declassified in Part - Sanitized Copy Approved for Release 2016/06/14 : CIA-RDP79T00936A009100160001-9

Declassified in Part - Sanitized Copy Approved for Release 2016/06/14 : CIA-RDP79T00936A009100160001-9

CAMBODIA

50X1

The South Vietnamese - Cambodian task force moving up from the south along Route 4 is still in the vicinity of Stung Chhay pass.

50X1

in spite of supply shortages, the North Vietnamese 101D Regiment remains in the area and is attempting to slow the advance of the task force. Cambodian officials announced today that the task force moving from the north has taken Pich Nil pass, according to late press reports.

50X1
50X1

but the Cambodian units of the task force were only a few miles short of the pass earlier today. A spokesman in Phnom Penh claimed that the pass was occupied without enemy resistance.

The South Vietnamese Government has agreed to provide naval escorts and air cover for river convoys to and from Phnom Penh. The Cambodians will assign liaison officers to the South Vietnamese craft to coordinate fire support, and Cambodian troops will mount new operations to attempt to clear the river banks between Neak Luong and Phnom Penh. The first escorted convoy arrived in Phnom Penh yesterday without incident.

4

Declassified in Part - Sanitized Copy Approved for Release 2016/06/14 : CIA-RDP79T00936A009100160001-9

Declassified in Part - Sanitized Copy Approved for Release 2016/06/14 : CIA-RDP79T00936A009100160001-9

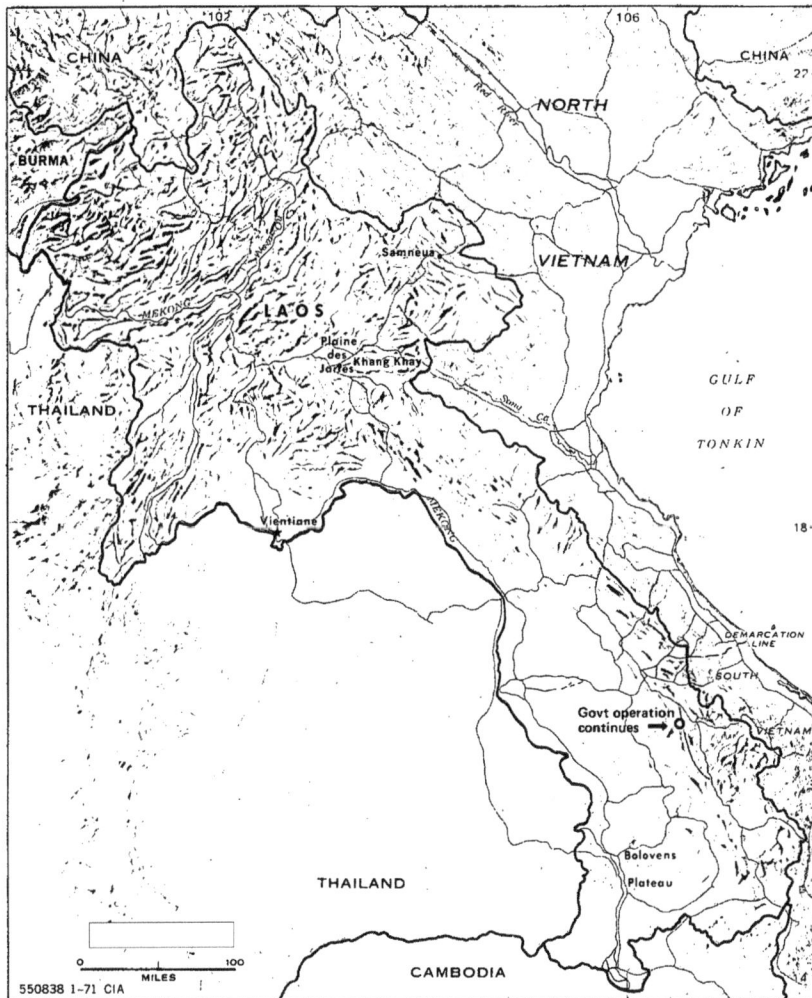

Declassified in Part - Sanitized Copy Approved for Release 2016/06/14 : CIA-RDP79T00936A009100160001-9

Declassified in Part - Sanitized Copy Approved for Release 2016/06/14 : CIA-RDP79T00936A009100160001-9

NOTES

Laos: Government forces pushing toward the new
Communist road in the infiltration corridor are encountering increased resistance. [   ]   50X1
[   ] the Communists are moving in forces to
counter the government forays. In the north, [   ]   50X1
[   ] the Communists' preoccupation with
supply shortages west of the Plaine des Jarres, and
indicate that elements of the North Vietnamese 312th
Division are now in the border area, perhaps inside
Laos. Meanwhile, Communist envoy Souk Vongsak has
advised Souvanna that he plans to go to Samneua late
this week for consultations, and assured him he will
return to Vientiane to resume discussions on possible
peace negotiations.

International Oil: Libya has given Occidental
and Bunker Hunt until today to respond to its demand
for increased oil revenues and mandatory reinvest-
ment of profits. The Libyans reject the companies'
position that they will negotiate only on the basis
of the industry-wide proposal presented on Saturday,
and the US Embassy believes that reprisals can be
expected if the companies stick to this stand. The
meeting between oil company negotiators and the Gulf
States negotiating committee is still scheduled for
tomorrow in Tehran.

Jordan: The cease-fire continues to hold, with
the movement of the fedayeen to bases outside of the
cities scheduled to be completed today. PFLP leader
Habbash's call for King Husayn's replacement by a
"popular, progressive, and nonreactionary" regime
points up the growing differences within the fedayeen ranks. A spokesman for the fedayeen central
committee retorted that the PFLP's actions repeatedly
provide the Jordanian Government with a pretext for
not adhering to agreements.

5

Declassified in Part - Sanitized Copy Approved for Release 2016/06/14 : CIA-RDP79T00936A009100160001-9

Declassified in Part - Sanitized Copy Approved for Release 2016/06/14 : CIA-RDP79T00936A009100160001-9

Top Secret

Declassified in Part - Sanitized Copy Approved for Release 2016/06/14 : CIA-RDP79T00936A009100160001-9

Declassified in Part - Sanitized Copy Approved for Release 2016/06/14 : CIA-RDP79T00936A009100170001-8

The President's Daily Brief

19 January 1971

48

Top Secret 50X1

Declassified in Part - Sanitized Copy Approved for Release 2016/06/14 : CIA-RDP79T00936A009100170001-8

Declassified in Part - Sanitized Copy Approved for Release 2016/06/14 : CIA-RDP79T00936A009100170001-8

THE PRESIDENT'S DAILY BRIEF

19 January 1971

PRINCIPAL DEVELOPMENTS

The North Vietnamese have moved two regimental head-quarters westward from the Ban Ban area of Laos to within ten miles of Muong Soui. *(Page 1)*

The press leak of Tokyo's plans to expand aid to Indochina undermines prospects for carrying out this policy. *(Page 2)*

Further work stoppages in Gdansk may account for Gierek's delay in setting a date for a central committee plenum he has announced. *(Page 3)*

On *Page 4* we report data on a new multipurpose Soviet destroyer.

	Soviet		Havana	50X1
	(Page 5)			
At Annex,			North	50X1
Vietnam				50X1

Declassified in Part - Sanitized Copy Approved for Release 2016/06/14 : CIA-RDP79T00936A009100170001-8

Declassified in Part - Sanitized Copy Approved for Release 2016/06/14 : CIA-RDP79T00936A009100170001-8

LAOS/PLAINE DES JARRES: Relocation of NVA Units

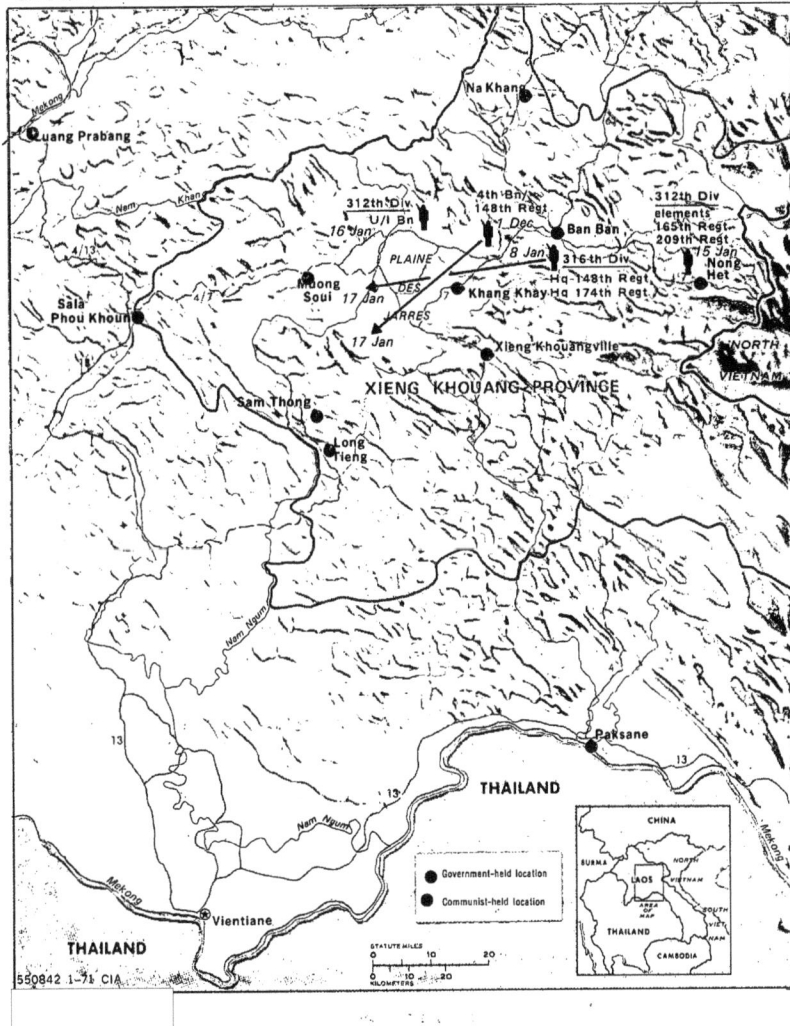

50X1

Declassified in Part - Sanitized Copy Approved for Release 2016/06/14 : CIA-RDP79T00936A009100170001-8

Declassified in Part - Sanitized Copy Approved for Release 2016/06/14 : CIA-RDP79T00936A009100170001-8

LAOS

The headquarters of two regiments from the North Vietnamese 316th Division--the 148th and the 174th--recently moved westward from the Ban Ban area to within ten miles of Muong Soui. In addition, a battalion of the 148th which had been located west of Ban Ban has moved about 25 miles southwestward and onto the Plaine.

> *This is the first time these regimental headquarters have been this far west in the Plaine; their subordinate battalions, however, have been active in the area for months, bearing the weight of the fighting in northern Laos.*
>
> *Although the regimental headquarters may want merely to assume tighter control over their subordinates, their relocation could also be related to the return to Laos of the 312th Division from North Vietnam. Last year the 316th's headquarters and regiments shifted southward closer to the fighting when the 312th moved into Laos as a back-up force.*

On 15 January the 209th Regiment of the 312th Division was tentatively located near Nong Het, close to the North Vietnamese border. There is evidence that elements of the division's 165th Regiment are in the same area. Direction finding has already located one unidentified battalion from the 312th north of the Plaine des Jarres.

At a time when these moves are being made to strengthen their military position in Laos, the Communists on 14 January called again for talks between the Pathet Lao and the government. In making the call, the Pathet Lao scaled down their conditions for starting talks at Khang Khay, citing the need to "de-escalate" bombing and air activity in Xieng Khouang Province but stopping short of demanding a complete cessation.

1

Declassified in Part - Sanitized Copy Approved for Release 2016/06/14 : CIA-RDP79T00936A009100170001-8

Declassified in Part - Sanitized Copy Approved for Release 2016/06/14 : CIA-RDP79T00936A009100170001-8

JAPAN-INDOCHINA

Details of Tokyo's plan to expand aid to the countries of Indochina have been leaked to a major Japanese newspaper. Included in the story is information about a secret understanding between Foreign Minister Aichi and Finance Minister Fukuda to use government reserve funds rather than a budget appropriation for grants to Cambodia.

50X1

Only recently, partly in response to US prodding and partly in the belief that the fighting is now on the wane, has there been growing sentiment in the Foreign Ministry and elsewhere in the government to expand aid to Indochina. Previously, Tokyo's policy had been to limit its assistance to small, "humanitarian" projects and to put off any significant increase until the hostilities end. The press leak, in addition to undermining the prospect of a shift in aid policy this year, may give the government's leftist critics a new opportunity to attack its association with US policy in Southeast Asia.

2

Declassified in Part - Sanitized Copy Approved for Release 2016/06/14 : CIA-RDP79T00936A009100170001-8

Declassified in Part - Sanitized Copy Approved for Release 2016/06/14 : CIA-RDP79T00936A009100170001-8

POLAND

Shipyard workers in Gdansk staged work stoppages the past two days and are threatening more today in support of economic and political demands. The strikers again called for Gierek or Premier Jaroszewicz to come to Gdansk for face-to-face discussions. The workers are also reported to be demanding the ouster of two politburo members: Mieczyslaw Moczar, whom they believe to have been responsible for the initial harsh antiriot measures last month; and Stanislaw Kociolek, a former Gdansk party leader whom Gierek has made responsible for economic affairs. Their economic complaints center on higher production targets which the workers say outweigh a rather limited range of benefits, including wage increases and free hot lunches during the winter.

> *The persistence of tension in Gdansk presumably is one reason why Gierek has so far failed to announce a firm date for the central committee plenum he has said would be held later this month. The plenum is slated to include a self-critical party appraisal of the "December events" and a program for future economic development. This agenda would be especially difficult without a settlement in Gdansk.*

3

Declassified in Part - Sanitized Copy Approved for Release 2016/06/14 : CIA-RDP79T00936A009100170001-8

Declassified in Part - Sanitized Copy Approved for Release 2016/06/14 : CIA-RDP79T00936A009100170001-8

New Multipurpose Soviet Destroyer

FINLAND
SWEDEN
Baltic Sea
Kaliningrad
Moscow
POLAND
U. S. S. R.
Shipyards constructing Krivak-class guided missile destroyer
CZECHOSLOVAKIA
HUNGARY
YUGOSLAVIA
ROMANIA
Kerch
Black Sea

50X1

Krivak-class Guided Missile Destroyer

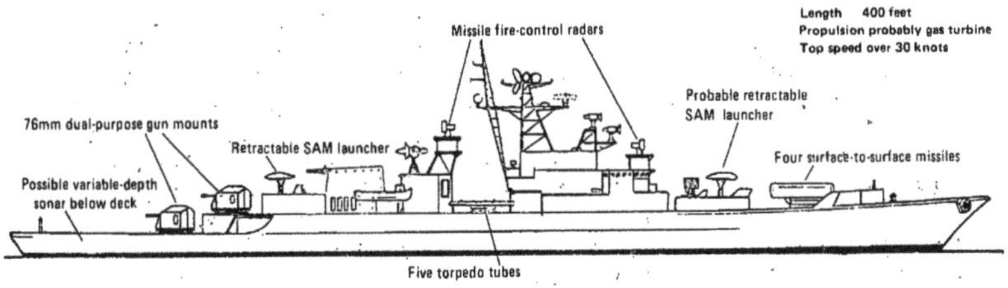
Length 400 feet
Propulsion probably gas turbine
Top speed over 30 knots
Missile fire-control radars
Probable retractable SAM launcher
76mm dual-purpose gun mounts
Retractable SAM launcher
Four surface-to-surface missiles
Possible variable-depth sonar below deck
Five torpedo tubes

550834 1-71 CIA

Declassified in Part - Sanitized Copy Approved for Release 2016/06/14 : CIA-RDP79T00936A009100170001-8

Declassified in Part - Sanitized Copy Approved for Release 2016/06/14 : CIA-RDP79T00936A009100170001-8

USSR

A new multipurpose Soviet destroyer has been photographed while on sea trials in the Baltic. This Krivak-class ship is about 400 feet long and carries surface-to-air missiles, surface-to-surface missiles, antisubmarine rockets, torpedoes, and dual-purpose naval guns.

The new destroyer appears designed primarily for antisubmarine warfare, but it is capable of attacking other surface ships with cruise missiles and of defending itself against air attack.

Satellite photography revealed the first ship of this class under construction at Kaliningrad on the Baltic in the fall of 1968.

50X1

The destroyer is also being built at Kerch on the Black Sea. Our information on this building program suggests that as many as 45 units could be completed during the 1970s. This would be the Soviets' largest construction program for naval surface ships since the Skoryy-class destroyers were built in the early 1950s.

4

Declassified in Part - Sanitized Copy Approved for Release 2016/06/14 : CIA-RDP79T00936A009100170001-8

Declassified in Part - Sanitized Copy Approved for Release 2016/06/14 : CIA-RDP79T00936A009100170001-8

USSR-CUBA

50X1

50X1

50X1

50X1

Declassified in Part - Sanitized Copy Approved for Release 2016/06/14 : CIA-RDP79T00936A009100170001-8

Declassified in Part - Sanitized Copy Approved for Release 2016/06/14 : CIA-RDP79T00936A0091100170001-8

NOTES

USSR: 50X1
                                                                    50X1

                                                                    50X1

                                                            50X1

                                                                    50X1
                                                                    50X1

USSR–Sudan: 50X1
                                                                    50X1

                                                                    50X1

Declassified in Part - Sanitized Copy Approved for Release 2016/06/14 : CIA-RDP79T00936A0091100170001-8

Declassified in Part - Sanitized Copy Approved for Release 2016/06/14 : CIA-RDP79T00936A009100170001-8

NORTH VIETNAMESE

50X1

50X1

A
N
N
E
X

(continued)

A-1

Declassified in Part - Sanitized Copy Approved for Release 2016/06/14 : CIA-RDP79T00936A009100170001-8

Declassified in Part - Sanitized Copy Approved for Release 2016/06/14 : CIA-RDP79T00936A009100170001-8

50X1

50X1

50X1

50X1

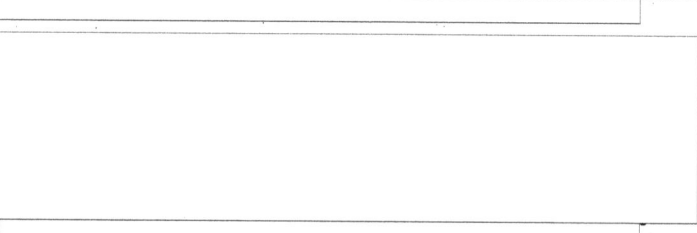

50X1

50X1

A-2

Declassified in Part - Sanitized Copy Approved for Release 2016/06/14 : CIA-RDP79T00936A009100170001-8

Declassified in Part - Sanitized Copy Approved for Release 2016/06/14 : CIA-RDP79T00936A009100170001-8

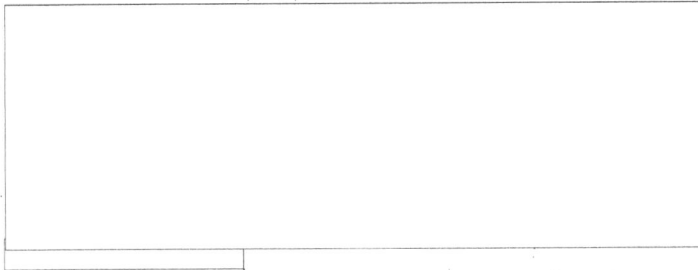

50X1

50X1

A-3

Declassified in Part - Sanitized Copy Approved for Release 2016/06/14 : CIA-RDP79T00936A009100170001-8

Declassified in Part - Sanitized Copy Approved for Release 2016/06/14 : CIA-RDP79T00936A009100170001-8

Top Secret

Declassified in Part - Sanitized Copy Approved for Release 2016/06/14 : CIA-RDP79T00936A009100170001-8

Declassified in Part - Sanitized Copy Approved for Release 2016/06/14 : CIA-RDP79T00936A009100180001-7

The President's Daily Brief

20 January 1971

48

Top Secret 50X1

Declassified in Part - Sanitized Copy Approved for Release 2016/06/14 : CIA-RDP79T00936A009100180001-7

Declassified in Part - Sanitized Copy Approved for Release 2016/06/14 : CIA-RDP79T00936A009100180001-7

FOR THE PRESIDENT ONLY

THE PRESIDENT'S DAILY BRIEF

20 January 1971

PRINCIPAL DEVELOPMENTS

On *Page 1* we provide highlights from the [   ] most recent assessment of the situation in Cambodia.

50X1

50X1

New photography shows little recent progress in Chinese road construction in northwest Laos. *(Page 2)*

Labor unrest persists in the Gdansk area of Poland. *(Page 3)*

Differences within the fedayeen movement are becoming more apparent as the quiet continues in Jordan. *(Page 4)*

FOR THE PRESIDENT ONLY

Declassified in Part - Sanitized Copy Approved for Release 2016/06/14 : CIA-RDP79T00936A009100180001-7

Declassified in Part - Sanitized Copy Approved for Release 2016/06/14 : CIA-RDP79T00936A009100180001-7

CAMBODIA

[ ]   50X1

[ ] *there is no evi-
dence of any serious deterioration in the morale of
the population in Phnom Penh. In spite of growing
hardships imposed by the shortages of petroleum and
the increase in consumer prices, there is no audible
grumbling over the way the war is going or the qual-
ity of leadership provided by Lon Nol or the gener-
als.* [ ] *some observers*   50X1
sense a growing malaise in the capital, but [ ]   50X1
[ ] *even if the city were to be totally cut off,*   50X1
*the life of the average Phnom Penh resident would
probably be little changed. Despite the events of
the past two months, there is still little sense of
war atmosphere or urgency in Phnom Penh; the most
readily apparent reason for this is the supreme confidence of the Cambodians that, if properly armed,
one Khmer is worth three Vietnamese, and therefore
time is on the side of the Cambodians.*

*Although police procedures have been tightened and
some terrorists arrested, Phnom Penh is still quite
vulnerable to enemy mortar or rocket harassment and
to acts of terrorism and sabotage. In the country-
side, the Vietnamese Communists are having more suc-
cess among the Cambodian population than the government admits, although reports of incidents between
the peasants and their would-be recruiters indicate
that the enemy also has serious troubles.*

*With the continuing help of the South Vietnamese,
and the increasing availability of new weapons and
trained troops, the Cambodian Army should perform
better in the coming months.* [ ]   50X1
[ ] *the exceedingly cautious*   50X1
*tactics employed by the Cambodians, which have en-
abled the Communists to retain the initiative, will
change until such time as field officers develop
greater experience and confidence, and Lon Nol stops
making most tactical decisions himself.*

1

Declassified in Part - Sanitized Copy Approved for Release 2016/06/14 : CIA-RDP79T00936A009100180001-7

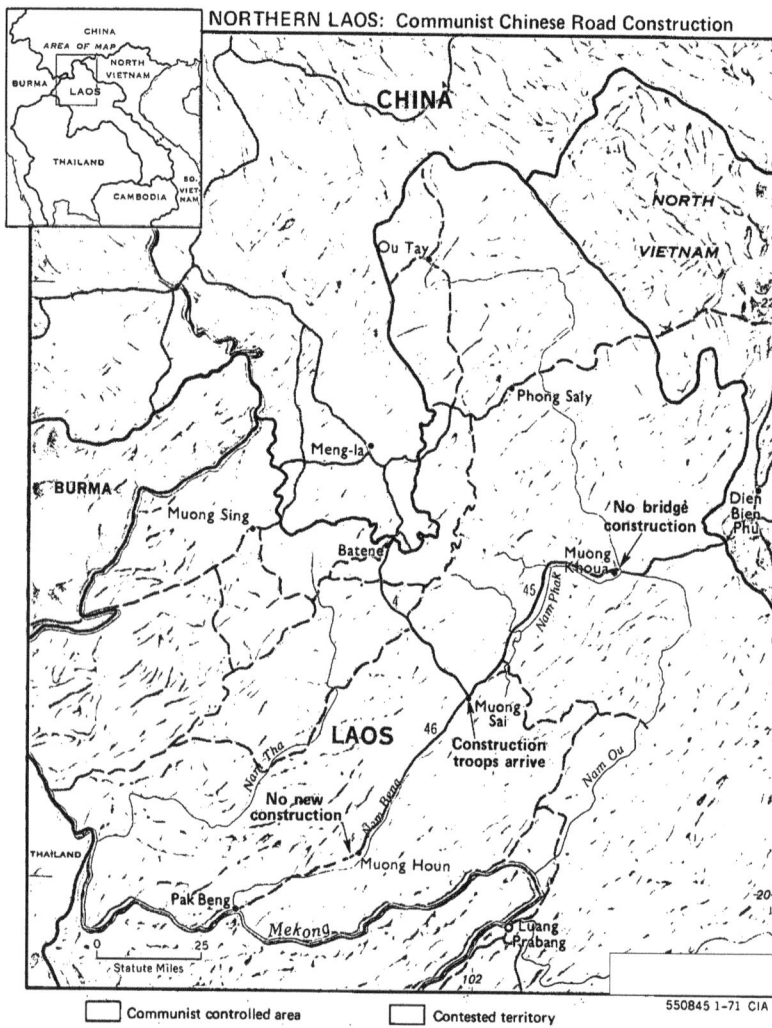

NORTHERN LAOS: Communist Chinese Road Construction

CHINA
AREA OF MAP
NORTH VIETNAM
BURMA
LAOS
THAILAND
SO. VIET-NAM
CAMBODIA

CHINA

Ou Tay

NORTH

VIETNAM

Phong Saly

Meng-la

No bridge construction

BURMA

Muong Sing

Dien Bien Phu

Bateng

Muong Khoua

45

Nam Phak

LAOS

46

Muong Sai

Construction troops arrive

Nam Beng

Nam Tha

Nam Ou

No new construction

THAILAND

Muong Houn

Pak Beng

-20

Mekong

Luang Prabang

0   25
Statute Miles

102

550845 1-71 CIA

☐ Communist controlled area   ☐ Contested territory

50X1

Declassified in Part - Sanitized Copy Approved for Release 2016/06/14 : CIA-RDP79T00936A009100180001-7

COMMUNIST CHINA - LAOS

Photography [   ] showed that Chinese   50X1
road construction in northwest Laos made little
progress over the last month. Construction to the
northeast--in the direction of North Vietnam--has
reached the Nam Ou River at Muong Khoua, but there
is no evidence that bridge or ferry construction
has begun. There has been no further road construction southwest toward the Mekong River since the extension of a motorable trail a few miles south of
Muong Houn, which we reported in The President's
Daily Brief of 3 December.

> *The fact that little construction has oc-
> curred recently may be due to a rotation
> of forces, which seems to occur annually
> at about this time.* [   ]   50X1
> *have reported the arrival in the Muong
> Sai area since mid-December of 2,000 new
> construction troops, apparently part of
> this rotation process.*

> *We estimate that the Chinese now have
> about 14,000 to 18,000 troops--mostly in
> engineer and AAA units--spread along the
> road system in northwest Laos. The in-
> crease of about 4,000 above early Decem-
> ber figures is due to the confirmed ad-
> dition of one new construction regiment
> since last fall and to revised strength
> estimates for such regiments, as well as
> for AAA units in the area.*

2

Declassified in Part - Sanitized Copy Approved for Release 2016/06/14 : CIA-RDP79T00936A009100180001-7

Declassified in Part - Sanitized Copy Approved for Release 2016/06/14 : CIA-RDP79T00936A009100180001-7

POLAND

Labor unrest persists in the Gdansk area. Most shipyard workers returned to work yesterday, but there was a brief work stoppage by public transport employees. A joint delegation of management and workers from the Gdansk shipyards met yesterday with Gierek and Premier Jaroszewicz in Warsaw to discuss the economic and political grievances of the workers.

A ranking Polish economist confirmed to US officials in Warsaw that a central committee plenum, to be held by late January or early February, is expected to set new guidelines for political, economic, and social policies, and to make additional personnel changes. He indicated that the plenum will chart a broad course of economic reform, but that specific changes are still being debated.

> *The party undoubtedly would like to see more evidence of popular backing and calm before setting the plenum date. The workers, however, have tasted power in toppling the old regime and are stubbornly insisting on a clear outline of the future before they give their support. Although Gierek seems determined to tackle basic economic and social shortcomings, his resources for satisfying the workers' immediate bread-and-butter grievances are no greater than Gomulka's. Gierek also knows that he cannot be forever beholden to the workers and that he must soon show the Polish populace, and the Soviets, that he is in charge of his own house.*

3

Declassified in Part - Sanitized Copy Approved for Release 2016/06/14 : CIA-RDP79T00936A009100180001-7

Declassified in Part - Sanitized Copy Approved for Release 2016/06/14 : CIA-RDP79T00936A009100180001-7

NOTE

Jordan-Fedayeen: The government continues to collect arms from various fedayeen militia groups-- including George Habbash's violence-prone Popular Front for the Liberation of Palestine (PFLP)--without incident. Meanwhile, divided loyalties within the fedayeen movement are becoming more apparent.

50X1

50X1

4

Declassified in Part - Sanitized Copy Approved for Release 2016/06/14 : CIA-RDP79T00936A009100180001-7

Declassified in Part - Sanitized Copy Approved for Release 2016/06/14 : CIA-RDP79T00936A009100180001-7

Top Secret

Declassified in Part - Sanitized Copy Approved for Release 2016/06/14 : CIA-RDP79T00936A009100180001-7

Declassified in Part - Sanitized Copy Approved for Release 2016/06/14 : CIA-RDP79T00936A009100190001-6

The President's Daily Brief

21 January 1971

50X1

50

Top Secret

Declassified in Part - Sanitized Copy Approved for Release 2016/06/14 : CIA-RDP79T00936A009100190001-6

FOR THE PRESIDENT ONLY

THE PRESIDENT'S DAILY BRIEF

21 January 1971

PRINCIPAL DEVELOPMENTS

In return for postponing their appeal to the Security Council, Egyptian leaders apparently hope to receive additional assurances that Israel will be more forth-coming in the peace talks. *(Page 1)*

The Soviets continue to be unyielding at the four-power ambassadorial talks on Berlin. *(Page 2)*

Venezuela   Cuba.
(Page 3)

50X1 50X1

50X1

Philippine authorities are preparing for student vio-lence next week. *(Page 4)*

FOR THE PRESIDENT ONLY

MIDDLE EAST

Foreign Minister Riad told Minister Bergus in
Cairo Tuesday that President Sadat and he had decided
to postpone their planned call for a Security Council
meeting. According to Riad, the decision was taken
as a response to the letter from Secretary Rogers
which the Egyptians claim indicates that the US "must
have something in mind or intends to do something."
Riad said that Soviet President Podgornyy had been
informed of their decision and had concurred in it.

> *The Egyptians obviously are trying to trade
> their decision to back off from an immediate
> Security Council meeting in return for in-
> creased US pressure on Israel. Cairo's de-
> cision apparently was made several days ago.*

50X1

Jarring told Ambassador Yost on 19 January that
he was working on a "third paper" containing his own
ideas. An object of the paper--which he planned to
have in the parties' hands by yesterday--was to ob-
tain a more explicit statement from Israel on withdrawal.

> *Jarring believes he needs something more
> forthcoming from Israel on withdrawal to
> avoid a Security Council meeting and to
> obtain an extension of the cease-fire.
> Israeli Ambassador Tekoah has told Jarring,
> however, that Israel cannot be more spe-
> cific on withdrawal at this time. He claimed
> this was Israel's most difficult domestic
> issue and could break up the government.*

1

Declassified in Part - Sanitized Copy Approved for Release 2016/06/14 : CIA-RDP79T00936A009100190001-6

USSR-BERLIN

At the four-power ambassadorial meeting on Tuesday, Abrasimov reiterated that Moscow is not prepared to negotiate any substantive improvement in existing access procedures. He also warned that "illegal" West German activities in West Berlin-- where an FDP party conclave is scheduled for 29-30 January--would bring retaliation, presumably a resumption of East German harassment of autobahn traffic.

> *Moscow's rigidity seems directly related to its long-held position that Berlin's problems should be solved in direct talks between Bonn and Pankow. Thus, the Kremlin wishes to deflect as many substantive issues as possible to that bilateral forum.*

Declassified in Part - Sanitized Copy Approved for Release 2016/06/14 : CIA-RDP79T00936A009100190001-6

Declassified in Part - Sanitized Copy Approved for Release 2016/06/14 : CIA-RDP79T00936A009100190001-6

VENEZUELA-CUBA

50X1

50X1

50X1

.50X1

50X1

50X1

50X1

3

Declassified in Part - Sanitized Copy Approved for Release 2016/06/14 : CIA-RDP79T00936A009100190001-6

Declassified in Part - Sanitized Copy Approved for Release 2016/06/14 : CIA-RDP79T00936A009100190001-6

NOTES

Philippines: Manila is bracing for student
demonstrations early next week. Marcos gives his
state of the nation address on Monday, and the following day is the anniversary of last year's student
disruptions. Military forces in the city, recently
augmented, now number over 6,000, and Marcos is considering the imposition of martial law. ⎵⎵⎵⎵⎵⎵⎵⎵⎵⎵⎵⎵
⎵⎵⎵⎵⎵⎵⎵⎵⎵⎵⎵⎵⎵⎵⎵⎵⎵⎵⎵⎵⎵⎵ the radicals' plans include
a march on the American Embassy.

50X1

Ecuador: The Foreign Ministry reacted to the
announced curtailment of US military aid by issuing
a communiqué yesterday accusing the US of violating
the sentiment of the OAS charter. Ambassador Burns
met with the foreign minister yesterday, however,
and was left with the impression that the government
would like to avoid any further incidents. The government's restraint does not necessarily apply to
President Velasco, who has acted without advice and
consent before ⎵⎵⎵⎵⎵⎵⎵⎵⎵⎵⎵⎵⎵⎵⎵⎵⎵⎵⎵ and
in a moment of pique he might go so far as to request the withdrawal of some US personnel or ex-
propriate a public utility owned by US interests.

50X1

4

Declassified in Part - Sanitized Copy Approved for Release 2016/06/14 : CIA-RDP79T00936A009100190001-6

Declassified in Part - Sanitized Copy Approved for Release 2016/06/14 : CIA-RDP79T00936A009100190001-6

Top Secret

Declassified in Part - Sanitized Copy Approved for Release 2016/06/14 : CIA-RDP79T00936A009100190001-6

Declassified in Part - Sanitized Copy Approved for Release 2016/06/14 : CIA-RDP79T00936A009100200001-4

The President's Daily Brief

22 January 1971

48

Top Secret 50X1

Declassified in Part - Sanitized Copy Approved for Release 2016/06/14 : CIA-RDP79T00936A009100200001-4

Declassified in Part - Sanitized Copy Approved for Release 2016/06/14 : CIA-RDP79T00936A009100200001-4

THE PRESIDENT'S DAILY BRIEF

22 January 1971

PRINCIPAL DEVELOPMENTS

Communist supply movements in the Laotian panhandle
increased sharply in early January. *(Page 1)*

50X1

(Page 2)   50X1

50X1

(Page 3)   50X1

Declassified in Part - Sanitized Copy Approved for Release 2016/06/14 : CIA-RDP79T00936A009100200001-4

Communists Moving Supplies Via Gulf of Thailand

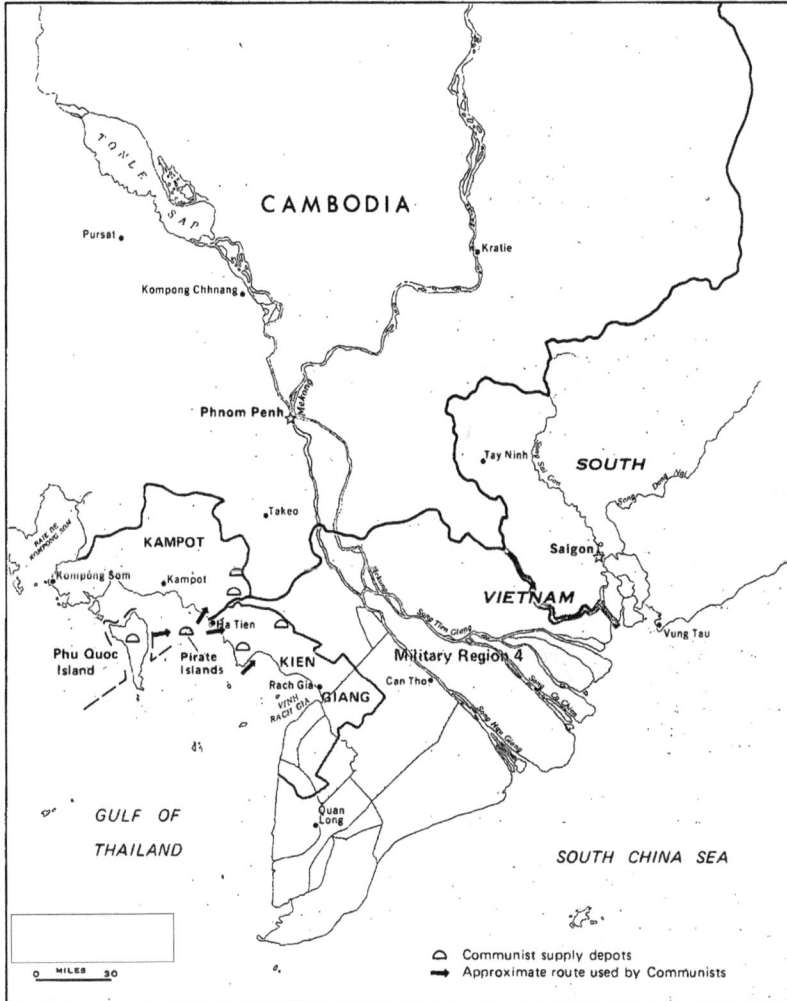

CAMBODIA

Pursat

Kratie

Kompong Chhnang

Phnom Penh

Tay Ninh

SOUTH

Takeo

KAMPOT

Saigon

Kompong Som

Kampot

VIETNAM

Ha Tien

Vung Tau

Phu Quoc
Island

Pirate
Islands

KIEN

Military Region 4

Rach Gia

Can Tho

GIANG

Quan
Long

GULF OF

THAILAND

SOUTH CHINA SEA

50X1

TONLE SAP

○ Communist supply depots
➡ Approximate route used by Communists

0   MILES   30

550843 1-71 CIA

Declassified in Part - Sanitized Copy Approved for Release 2016/06/14 : CIA-RDP79T00936A009100200001-4

INDOCHINA

The flow of supplies between two important logistic units in the Laotian panhandle averaged at least 180 tons nightly in the first ten days of January, according to a recent message. This is about two and a half times the rate moved in December 1970 and is the highest ever detected between two rear service units.

> *With the closing of Kompong Som (Sihanoukville), we have expected the Communists to mount an expanded logistics effort via the panhandle this dry season. Supply activity should remain at a high level throughout the panhandle for the next several months.*

* * *

The Communists are moving small amounts of supplies by sea into southern South Vietnam and Cambodia, according to clandestine sources. Munitions and other supplies move by motorized junks from Phu Quoc Island in the Gulf of Thailand to the Pirate Islands, about nine miles off the coast. In the Pirate Islands supplies are transferred to shallow-draft sampans which travel up the maze of rivers to major supply depots in Kampot Province, Cambodia, and in Kien Giang Province, South Vietnam.

> *The areas allegedly being supplied by sea are far removed from the main logistic route through southern Laos. Furthermore, the last deliveries to the delta via Kompong Som occurred in January 1970, and since the allied cross-border operations last spring there have been several reports of ammunition shortages in the delta.*

> *The enemy has traditionally been able to shuttle some supplies along the coast in sampans and junks. Supplies at Phu Quoc Island could get to the mainland in this manner. The US Navy maintains a detection system off the coast, however, and it seems unlikely that the Communists could move large quantities of supplies in from the open sea to Phu Quoc Island.*

1

Declassified in Part - Sanitized Copy Approved for Release 2016/06/14 : CIA-RDP79T00936A009100200001-4

Declassified in Part - Sanitized Copy Approved for Release 2016/06/14 : CIA-RDP79T00936A009100200001-4

THAILAND

50X1

50X1

50X1

50X1

50X1

50X1

50X1

50X1

50X1

2

Declassified in Part - Sanitized Copy Approved for Release 2016/06/14 : CIA-RDP79T00936A009100200001-4

Declassified in Part - Sanitized Copy Approved for Release 2016/06/14 : CIA-RDP79T00936A009100200001-4

USSR

50X1

50X1

3

Declassified in Part - Sanitized Copy Approved for Release 2016/06/14 : CIA-RDP79T00936A009100200001-4

Declassified in Part - Sanitized Copy Approved for Release 2016/06/14 : CIA-RDP79T00936A009100200001-4

NOTES

50X1

USSR: 50X1
50X1

50X1

4

Declassified in Part - Sanitized Copy Approved for Release 2016/06/14 : CIA-RDP79T00936A009100200001-4

Declassified in Part - Sanitized Copy Approved for Release 2016/06/14 : CIA-RDP79T00936A009100200001-4

Top Secret

Declassified in Part - Sanitized Copy Approved for Release 2016/06/14 : CIA-RDP79T00936A009100200001-4

Declassified in Part - Sanitized Copy Approved for Release 2016/06/14 : CIA-RDP79T00936A009100210001-3

The President's Daily Brief

23 January 1971

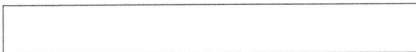

47

Top Secret

50X1

Declassified in Part - Sanitized Copy Approved for Release 2016/06/14 : CIA-RDP79T00936A009100210001-3

Declassified in Part - Sanitized Copy Approved for Release 2016/06/14 : CIA-RDP79T00936A009100210001-3

THE PRESIDENT'S DAILY BRIEF

23 January 1971

PRINCIPAL DEVELOPMENTS

On *Page 1* we comment on the Communist attacks near Phnom Penh yesterday morning.

Elements of North Vietnam's 312th Division continue to move westward in the Plaine des Jarres area. *(Page 2)*

On *Page 3* we discuss what appears to be a changing relationship between Poland's leaders and the Polish people.

Cuba	Guatemala		50X1X1
		(Page 4)	50X1
Page 5			50X1
			50X1

Declassified in Part - Sanitized Copy Approved for Release 2016/06/14 : CIA-RDP79T00936A009100210001-3

Declassified in Part - Sanitized Copy Approved for Release 2016/06/14 : CIA-RDP79T00936A009100210001-3

CAMBODIA

The Communists' attacks yesterday against the Phnom Penh airfield and other targets near the city are a major departure in their tactics in Cambodia. For the past ten months they have avoided taking the war directly to the capital, although they clearly have had the capability of doing so.

Although additional hit-and-run attacks on important targets in and around Phnom Penh can be expected, there are still no signs that the Communists are in a position to attack the city itself in force. The closest known Communist main force unit to Phnom Penh is the North Vietnamese 96th Artillery Regiment, which intercepts located 25 miles east-northeast of the capital on 20 January.

The government is taking increased security precautions to protect Pochentong Airfield and the city's power plants and petroleum depots. Sweep operations are under way in the outlying areas from which yesterday's mortar and sapper attacks were mounted. Lon Nol told Ambassador Swank yesterday that he plans to reinforce the capital's defenses with a trusted brigade of Khmer Krom troops currently involved in the Route 4 operation and with other troops now in the Skoun area.

Even in the face of these measures, the Communists can still make things a good deal tougher in the city if they are determined to shake the resolve of the Cambodian leadership or to bring into question the continuing viability of the Lon Nol regime. Some lower ranking military officers are already looking for scapegoats.

50X1

50X1

50X1

1

Declassified in Part - Sanitized Copy Approved for Release 2016/06/14 : CIA-RDP79T00936A009100210001-3

Declassified in Part - Sanitized Copy Approved for Release 2016/06/14 : CIA-RDP79T00936A009100210001-3

LAOS: Current Situation

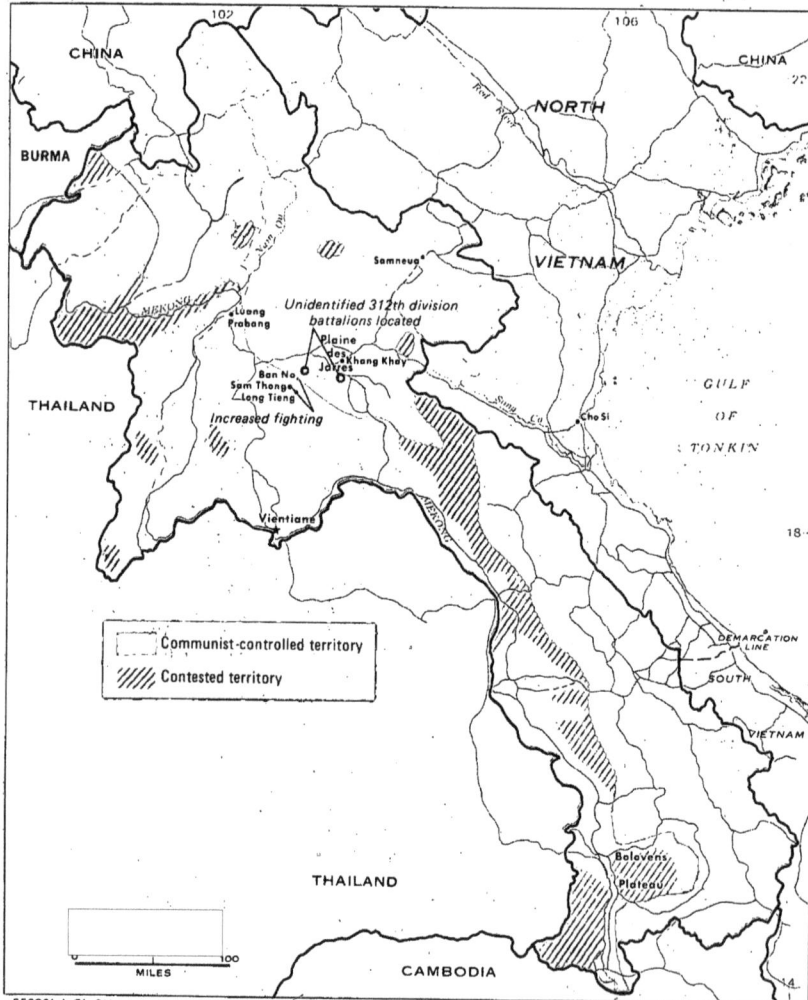

CHINA

CHINA

BURMA

NORTH VIETNAM

Samneua

Luang Prabang

Unidentified 312th division
battalions located

Plaine des Jarres

Xieng Khay

Ban Na
Sam Thong
Long Tieng

Increased fighting

THAILAND

Cho Si

GULF

OF

TONKIN

18

Vientiane

DEMARCATION LINE

SOUTH

VIETNAM

Communist-controlled territory

Contested territory

THAILAND

Bolovens
Plateau

MILES   100

CAMBODIA

550861 1-71 CIA

50X1

Declassified in Part - Sanitized Copy Approved for Release 2016/06/14 : CIA-RDP79T00936A009100210001-3

Declassified in Part - Sanitized Copy Approved for Release 2016/06/14 : CIA-RDP79T00936A009100210001-3

LAOS

An unidentified battalion of North Vietnam's 312th Division is now located west of the Plaine des Jarres. Another unidentified battalion, possibly associated with the division's 209th Regiment, now is located just south of Route 4 near the eastern edge of the Plaine. Elements of the division's 165th Regiment have asked a regiment of the 316th Division west of the Plaine for substantial quantities of ammunition, food, and medical supplies.

> *Elements of the 312th Division began passing through the Cho Si transshipment area in North Vietnam only a little more than two weeks ago. This rapid movement suggests that the Communists may hope to launch a campaign against the Long Tieng complex somewhat earlier than late February, the time of last year's drive. It is also possible that units of the 312th will spell units of the 316th Division, which has been on the front line continuously for almost two years. Last year the 312th was principally involved in rear-area operations, while the 316th made the major attack toward Long Tieng.*

In the last several days fighting has increased south and west of the Plaine, with a number of probes and skirmishes around Ban Na and Sam Thong. On 21 January, Communist forces overran a 40-man government outpost about eight miles northwest of Ban Na.

50X1

50X1

50X1

50X1

2

Declassified in Part - Sanitized Copy Approved for Release 2016/06/14 : CIA-RDP79T00936A009100210001-3

Declassified in Part - Sanitized Copy Approved for Release 2016/06/14 : CIA-RDP79T00936A009100210001-3

POLAND

The relationship between Poland's leaders and the populace appears to be in an important period of transition. The new leadership, not wishing to risk the resumption of violent disorders, has renounced force as a way of responding to the people's demands. Instead, it appears to have made a conscious decision to allow grievances, many of long standing, to surface and be catalogued for correction.

This decision has meant the tacit acceptance of work slowdowns and the consequent loss of production as the legitimate bargaining tools of the workers. There have been no reports of penalties being imposed on workers involved in such actions, and security authorities and the police have kept a low profile since the end of the riots. The only demands made on the workers by the controlled press-- and these have not been rigidly defined--have been that criticisms and calls for changes be constructive and feasible.

The new leaders' style seems to have given the Polish people a new sense of self-assurance. The workers on the Baltic coast exhibit an ever-growing confidence that the time has come, after years of tolerance on their part, to correct many of the faults endemic to Gomulka's leadership. If they did not have hopes of convincing the new leaders that this must be done, they would not be negotiating with local authorities and the new officials in Warsaw. Rather they would by now either have returned to sullen apathy or renewed rioting.

There also are signs that the workers' new-found pluckiness has spread to other strata of society. Students in Szczecin, for example, have recently demanded better conditions for study and life. The Polish people do not have wild revolutionary ambitions, but they have demonstrated a strong need to vent pent-up frustrations and to seek real improvements within the system. Poland's new leaders seem to recognize that it would be imprudent to block this safety valve at this time.

The dangers for the new leaders in such a course are obvious, and they have not hidden their need for time to plan changes, assign priorities, and find the proper people to carry out reforms. Their low-key approach indicates not only a desire gradually to restore calm, but also the pressure of time. There are fresh reports that the party central committee will meet next week in a pivotal session.

3

Declassified in Part - Sanitized Copy Approved for Release 2016/06/14 : CIA-RDP79T00936A009100210001-3

Declassified in Part - Sanitized Copy Approved for Release 2016/06/14 : CIA-RDP79T00936A009100210001-3

CUBA-GUATEMALA

50X1

50X1

50X1

50X1

50X1

4

Declassified in Part - Sanitized Copy Approved for Release 2016/06/14 : CIA-RDP79T00936A009100210001-3

Declassified in Part - Sanitized Copy Approved for Release 2016/06/14 : CIA-RDP79T00936A009100210001-3

JORDAN

50X1

50X1
50X1

50X1
50X1

50X1

5

50X1

Declassified in Part - Sanitized Copy Approved for Release 2016/06/14 : CIA-RDP79T00936A009100210001-3

Declassified in Part - Sanitized Copy Approved for Release 2016/06/14 : CIA-RDP79T00936A009100210001-3

NOTE

USSR:

50X1
50X1

6.

Declassified in Part - Sanitized Copy Approved for Release 2016/06/14 : CIA-RDP79T00936A009100210001-3

Declassified in Part - Sanitized Copy Approved for Release 2016/06/14 : CIA-RDP79T00936A009100210001-3

Top Secret

Declassified in Part - Sanitized Copy Approved for Release 2016/06/14 : CIA-RDP79T00936A009100210001-3

Declassified in Part - Sanitized Copy Approved for Release 2016/06/14 : CIA-RDP79T00936A009100220001-2

The President's Daily Brief

25 January 1971

46

Top Secret 50X1

Declassified in Part - Sanitized Copy Approved for Release 2016/06/14 : CIA-RDP79T00936A009100220001-2

Declassified in Part - Sanitized Copy Approved for Release 2016/06/14 : CIA-RDP79T00936A0091002220001-2

THE PRESIDENT'S DAILY BRIEF

25 January 1971

PRINCIPAL DEVELOPMENTS

In Cambodia, the enemy continues to employ small harassing attacks and terrorist tactics in and around Phnom Penh. *(Page 1)*

Poland's new leaders made several moves over the weekend to correct the country's labor unrest. *(Page 2)*

Hanoi is still augmenting its forces along both sides of the North Vietnam - Laos border. *(Page 4)*

South Korea [   ]   50X1
[   ] South Vietnam. *(Page 5)*   50X1

Enemy military activity in South Vietnam is expected to be light during the Tet cease-fire. *(Page 6)*

Declassified in Part - Sanitized Copy Approved for Release 2016/06/14 : CIA-RDP79T00936A0091002220001-2

CAMBODIA: Current Situation

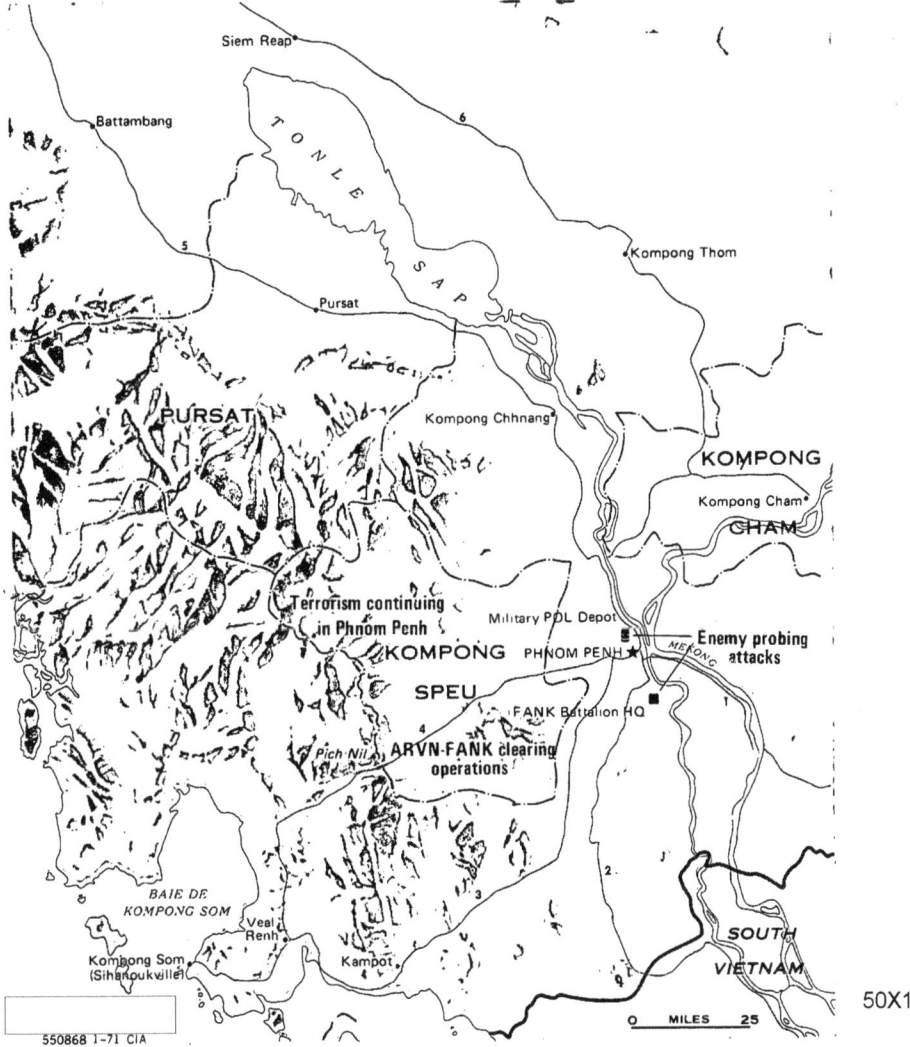

Siem Reap

Battambang

TONLE SAP

6

5

Kompong Thom

Pursat

Kompong Chhnang

PURSAT

KOMPONG

Kompong Cham

CHAM

Terrorism continuing
in Phnom Penh

Military POL Depot

KOMPONG

PHNOM PENH ★

Enemy probing
attacks

MEKONG

SPEU

FANK Battalion HQ

4

Pich Nil

ARVN-FANK clearing
operations

3

2

1

BAIE DE
KOMPONG SOM

Veal
Renh

SOUTH

Kompong Som
(Sihanoukville)

Kampot

VIETNAM

0   MILES   25

50X1

550868 1-71 CIA

Declassified in Part - Sanitized Copy Approved for Release 2016/06/14 : CIA-RDP79T00936A009100220001-2

CAMBODIA

In Phnom Penh, the third terrorist bombing incident in as many days destroyed a small building
next to an electric company office yesterday but did
not cause serious damage to any power facilities.
Last night the Pochentong airport received light
mortar or rocket fire and some automatic weapons
fire but there were no casualties or damage. Outside the capital, Communist probing attacks on a
military petroleum storage area just north of Phnom
Penh and against a government battalion several
miles southeast of the city were quickly repelled
over the weekend. The government has strengthened
Phnom Penh's defenses with five battalions from
Pursat and Kompong Speu provinces and has ordered
several other battalions now operating in the Route
6-7 sector in Kompong Cham Province to return to
the capital immediately.

> *The city's population has been concerned
> about the army's ability to protect them
> since the airfield raid last week, and
> these reinforcements may renew their con-
> fidence. The arrival of additional gov-
> ernment troops is not likely to discourage
> or prevent the Communists from carrying
> out additional harassing attacks and ter-
> rorist actions, however.*

Further west, Cambodian and South Vietnamese
forces are now engaged in clearing operations and
road repair on Route 4, following their linkup in
the Pich Nil pass area. The highway may be passable
for some traffic today. One South Vietnamese ranger
battalion has been airlifted back to South Vietnam,
and some Cambodian forces that helped secure the
north end of the pass are also anxious to return to
their home base.

1

Declassified in Part - Sanitized Copy Approved for Release 2016/06/14 : CIA-RDP79T00936A009100220001-2

Declassified in Part - Sanitized Copy Approved for Release 2016/06/14 : CIA-RDP79T00936A009100220001-2

POLAND

Polish authorities reacted promptly over the weekend to large-scale work stoppages in or around Szczecin. Party leader Gierek visited Szczecin yesterday afternoon to address a workers' meeting, and there were numerous flights of transport aircraft between 21 and 23 January from Warsaw to Goleniow, the military airfield nearest the port city.

There have been no reports of violence in Szczecin, but these planes may very well have carried police reinforcements in the event there is further trouble. Szczecin was one of the major areas of disorder during the rioting last month, and because of its proximity to the East German border, Poland's new leaders may have received some pressure from Ulbricht to make a special effort to keep the lid on Szczecin.

50X1

Gierek's trip to Szczecin may be the first in a series of face-to-face discussions with the workers in accordance with labor's demands.

50X1

50X1

50X1

50X1

50X1

(continued)

2

Declassified in Part - Sanitized Copy Approved for Release 2016/06/14 : CIA-RDP79T00936A009100220001-2

Declassified in Part - Sanitized Copy Approved for Release 2016/06/14 : CIA-RDP79T00936A009100220001-2

It was announced on Saturday that the minister of interior had requested and received a leave of absence for health reasons. The same day, however, Jaroszewicz submitted a motion to parliament calling for his ouster.

> *The outgoing minister appears to be the first scapegoat for the violence last month on the Baltic coast. The way his departure was handled suggests that a last minute decision was made not to let him down softly. The leadership may have reasoned that a "leave of absence" would not satisfy the workers and fired him outright.*

3

Declassified in Part - Sanitized Copy Approved for Release 2016/06/14 : CIA-RDP79T00936A009100220001-2

Declassified in Part - Sanitized Copy Approved for Release 2016/06/14 : CIA-RDP79T00936A009100220001-2

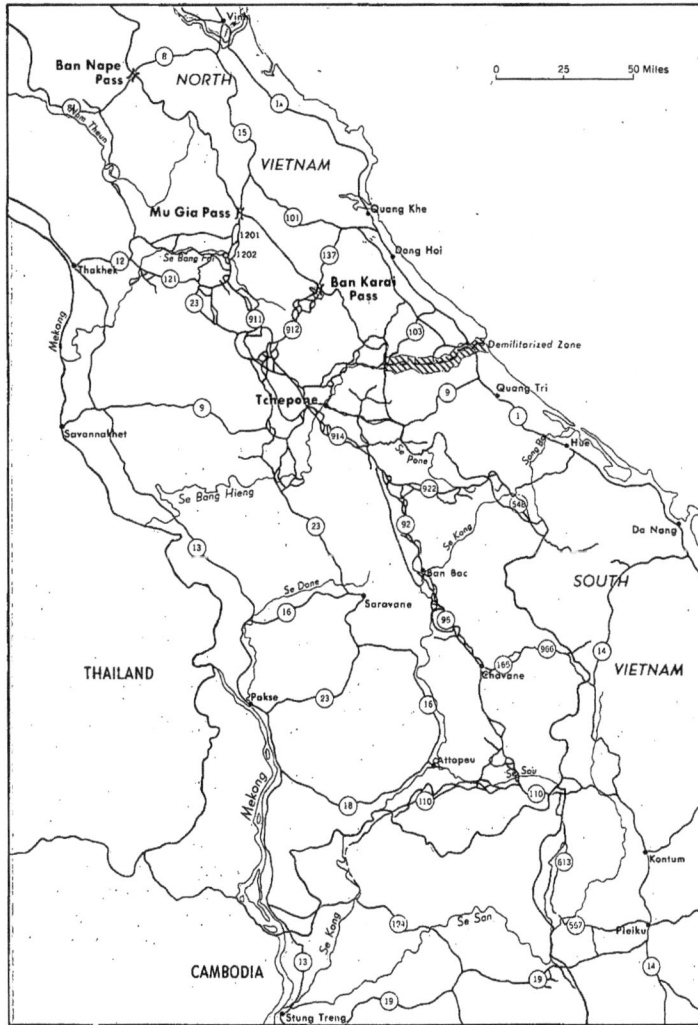

0   25   50 Miles

Ban Nape Pass
NORTH
VIETNAM
Mu Gia Pass
Quang Khe
Dong Hoi
Thakhek
Se Bang Fai
Ban Karai Pass
Demilitarized Zone
Tchepone
Quang Tri
Savannakhet
Hue
Se Pone
Song Bo
Se Bang Hieng
Se Kong
Da Nang
Se Done
Ban Bac
SOUTH
Saravane
THAILAND
Pakse
Chavane
VIETNAM
Attapeu
Se Sou
Kontum
Mekong
Se Kong
Se San
Pleiku
CAMBODIA
Stung Treng

550867 1-71

Declassified in Part - Sanitized Copy Approved for Release 2016/06/14 : CIA-RDP79T00936A009100220001-2

Declassified in Part - Sanitized Copy Approved for Release 2016/06/14 : CIA-RDP79T00936A009100220001-2

NORTH VIETNAM

Hanoi is continuing to strengthen its ground defenses in southern North Vietnam and in the Laotian panhandle to protect the significantly increased flow of supplies down the Ho Chi Minh trail.

The only elements of the North Vietnamese 320th Division still in North Vietnam, the division headquarters and the 64th Regiment, appear to be moving into the Laotian panhandle. A regiment from the 308th Division--the 102nd--has meanwhile joined the rest of the division in southern North Vietnam. The 308th has been moving steadily southward for several months from its garrison just below Hanoi. Intercepts indicate that the headquarters of the North Vietnamese 2nd Division is still in the Tchepone area of the Laos panhandle and not on its way back to South Vietnam.

These ground forces appear to be controlled by a major new headquarters, set up in southern North Vietnam last fall. The headquarters appears to be directing all units along the enemy's logistical network on both sides of the North Vietnam - Laos border and as far south as central South Vietnam.

4

Declassified in Part - Sanitized Copy Approved for Release 2016/06/14 : CIA-RDP79T00936A009100220001-2

Declassified in Part - Sanitized Copy Approved for Release 2016/06/14 : CIA-RDP79T00936A009100220001-2

SOUTH KOREA - SOUTH VIETNAM

50X1

50X1

50X1

50X1

50X1

50X1

5

Declassified in Part - Sanitized Copy Approved for Release 2016/06/14 : CIA-RDP79T00936A009100220001-2

Declassified in Part - Sanitized Copy Approved for Release 2016/06/14 : CIA-RDP79T00936A009100220001-2

TET CEASE-FIRE PERIODS
Tet Holiday January 27-29

		Saigon	Washington
Communist	Begins	Jan. 26-0100	Jan. 25-1200
	Ends	Jan. 30-0100	Jan. 29-1200
Allied	Begins	Jan. 26-1800	Jan. 26-0500
	Ends	Jan. 27-1800	Jan. 27-0500

550852 1-71

Declassified in Part - Sanitized Copy Approved for Release 2016/06/14 : CIA-RDP79T00936A009100220001-2

Declassified in Part - Sanitized Copy Approved for Release 2016/06/14 : CIA-RDP79T00936A009100220001-2

NOTES

South Vietnam: An analysis of reports indicates that the Communists will generally abide by their unilateral four-day Tet cease-fire which begins today. Preparations for post-Tet military action continue to surface, however. One enemy unit radioed recently that the next round of offensive activity is to begin the night of 31 January - 1 February--a day after the conclusion of the cease-fire. The northern provinces and the sector northwest of Saigon near the Cambodian border continue to be the most likely targets for enemy action.

Uganda: US Embassy officials report the heavy gunfire that echoed throughout Kampala last night had slackened by dawn. Tanks have been sighted on the streets, and the parliament building appears to be isolated. The military may have moved to unseat President Obote who has not yet returned from the Commonwealth conference in Singapore. On the other hand, the army is renowned for its poor discipline, and its many divisive factions may be settling some old scores among themselves.

6

Declassified in Part - Sanitized Copy Approved for Release 2016/06/14 : CIA-RDP79T00936A009100220001-2

Declassified in Part - Sanitized Copy Approved for Release 2016/06/14 : CIA-RDP79T00936A009100220001-2

Top Secret

Declassified in Part - Sanitized Copy Approved for Release 2016/06/14 : CIA-RDP79T00936A009100220001-2

Declassified in Part - Sanitized Copy Approved for Release 2016/06/14 : CIA-RDP79T00936A009100230001-1

The President's Daily Brief

26 January 1971

49

Top Secret

50X1

Declassified in Part - Sanitized Copy Approved for Release 2016/06/14 : CIA-RDP79T00936A009100230001-1

Declassified in Part - Sanitized Copy Approved for Release 2016/06/14 : CIA-RDP79T00936A009100230001-1

THE PRESIDENT'S DAILY BRIEF

26 January 1971

PRINCIPAL DEVELOPMENTS

The fedayeen are charging the Jordanian Government with violations of the latest cease-fire agreement. *(Page 1)*

Lon Nol and Sirik Matak appear to have retained their strong resolve despite the wave of terrorist incidents. *(Page 2)*

Army dissidents led by General Amin appear to be in control of the Ugandan capital following the coup yesterday. *(Page 3)*

Tokyo's attitude on Voice of America operations in Okinawa is another example of its growing independent approach in relations with the US. *(Page 4)*

The Polish Government has announced preparations for granting the Church legal title to former German church lands that are under regime control. *(Page 5)*

Declassified in Part - Sanitized Copy Approved for Release 2016/06/14 : CIA-RDP79T00936A009100230001-1

Declassified in Part - Sanitized Copy Approved for Release 2016/06/14 : CIA-RDP79T00936A009100230001-1

FEDAYEEN-JORDAN

The fedayeen central committee has charged that Jordanian authorities have failed to comply with the terms of the cease-fire of 13 January, although it claims the fedayeen fulfilled all their obligations by the deadline of 23 January. The central committee accuses the government of attempting to stir up an anti-fedayeen and anti-Palestinian campaign among the Jordanian public and of encouraging armed attacks on fedayeen offices in Jordan. Meanwhile, in a broadcast from Algeria, Yasir Arafat has claimed that Jordanian authorities are collaborating with the US and Israel to crush the guerrilla movement and force it to surrender to Israel. Arafat predicted the regime would not honor the latest cease-fire agreement and called for the dispatch of troops from other Arab countries to Jordan and its borders.

These accusations appear designed mainly to keep up morale among the frayed fedayeen groups in Jordan. Jordanian Premier Wasfi Tal has adopted a tough line in responding to the commandos, claiming the fedayeen are merely making excuses for the failure of their guerrilla campaign against Israel. He made it clear that the government would again use force if the commandos disrupted the present cease-fire agreement.

50X1

50X1

50X1

50X1

1

Declassified in Part - Sanitized Copy Approved for Release 2016/06/14 : CIA-RDP79T00936A009100230001-1

Declassified in Part - Sanitized Copy Approved for Release 2016/06/14 : CIA-RDP79T00936A009100230001-1

CAMBODIA

In a private meeting with Lon Nol and Sirik Matak yesterday, Ambassador Swank found them both in an excellent frame of mind. Lon Nol in particular exhibited his customary confidence and did not appear at all daunted by the incidents of sabotage and terrorism that followed the heavy attack on Pochentong airfield. Lon Nol said the enemy was in the process of being rooted out of the environs of the capital, and security of key installations was "being assured." *(Although the Cambodians are making an effort to secure the capital, it is unlikely--given their inexperience--that they can guarantee the safety of key points.)*

When Ambassador Swank asked for their reading of the political situation in Phnom Penh, both agreed that the populace is more apprehensive (Sirik Matak said, "War is no longer theoretical but real"), but they saw no weakening in public resolve to stand up against the enemy.

Ambassador Swank came away with the impression that their own strong resolve has not been weakened by recent events and that they remain convinced their cause ultimately will triumph. He notes that the hardships and the tragedy of war are now being brought home to the average Khmer in the capital, and that some intellectuals and the military already are searching for scapegoats. Ambassador Swank's judgment is that these trends do not currently have serious implications for the positions of these two leaders.

2

Declassified in Part - Sanitized Copy Approved for Release 2016/06/14 : CIA-RDP79T00936A009100230001-1

Declassified in Part - Sanitized Copy Approved for Release 2016/06/14 : CIA-RDP79T00936A009100230001-1

UGANDA

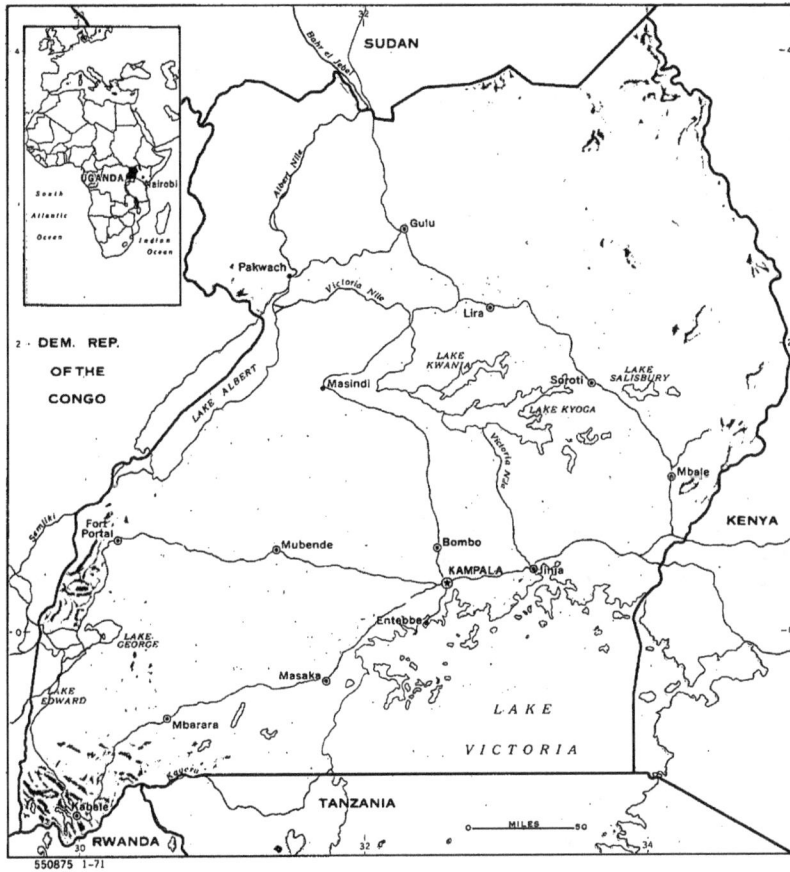

Declassified in Part - Sanitized Copy Approved for Release 2016/06/14 : CIA-RDP79T00936A009100230001-1

Declassified in Part - Sanitized Copy Approved for Release 2016/06/14 : CIA-RDP79T00936A009100230001-1

UGANDA

Army dissidents led by General Idi Amin appear to be in control of the Ugandan capital of Kampala following the coup yesterday against President Milton Obote. They effectively enforced a curfew in the capital last night and troops have closed the nearby airport at Entebbe. Radio Uganda is broadcasting statements claiming that Amin acted to rid the government of corruption and to restore public confidence. Amin describes his government as merely a caretaker administration and says he intends to return the government to civilian hands in due course.

The coup was clearly timed to coincide with Obote's absence at the Commonwealth conference in Singapore, but little is known yet about other circumstances of the take-over. It is not clear how much support Amin has, even within the army which is shot through with personal and tribal factionalism. Amin has been at odds with other senior officers and he may have acted with only a small number of supporters.

Rumors were widespread yesterday that Obote would try to return to the country, but he remained in Nairobi last night and there was no firm indication of his immediate plans. The situation could remain unstable for some time even if Obote does not return. Amin will be hard-pressed to handle the factionalism in the army, that only mirrors the tribal divisions within the country's general population.

Declassified in Part - Sanitized Copy Approved for Release 2016/06/14 : CIA-RDP79T00936A009100230001-1

Declassified in Part - Sanitized Copy Approved for Release 2016/06/14 : CIA-RDP79T00936A009100230001-1

JAPAN-OKINAWA

The latest example of Japan's growing independent approach in its relations with the US, as discussed in The President's Daily Brief Annex on 23 December, comes in Tokyo's response to the US request to allow Voice of America operations to continue after 1972 when the island is scheduled to revert to Japan.

The Japanese Government informed the US late last week that the Voice of America facilities will have to be removed upon reversion. In conveying this decision, a high Foreign Office official told the US Embassy that Japan was rejecting the US request not only because of laws forbidding foreign broadcasting from Japanese soil, but also because of long-standing public sensitivity to such activity. He added that it would be extremely difficult to build the political consensus necessary to amend the laws and that the political reaction would likely be serious if any amendments were "rammed through."

The official also cited fear of offending Communist China at a time of what he termed "delicate change" in the international situation. Every possible alternative had been considered, he claimed, but no formula had been found that would not create insurmountable domestic political problems.

4

Declassified in Part - Sanitized Copy Approved for Release 2016/06/14 : CIA-RDP79T00936A009100230001-1

Declassified in Part - Sanitized Copy Approved for Release 2016/06/14 : CIA-RDP79T00936A009100230001-1

NOTE

Poland: The government announced preparations
yesterday for granting the Roman Catholic Church
legal title to former German church lands that are
under regime control. Title would not revert to the
church before the Vatican has recognized Poland's
western border--a move that is unlikely until rati-
fication of the Polish - West German treaty--but the
announcement is an important gesture by the regime
toward reconciliation with the church. It will help
the government to enlist the support of the Polish
episcopate and is designed to improve in general its
standing with the strongly religious population.

*   *   *

Normal work appears to have resumed in areas
along the Baltic coast following the visit of party
leader Gierek and Premier Jaroszewicz to Szczecin
and Gdansk.

5

Declassified in Part - Sanitized Copy Approved for Release 2016/06/14 : CIA-RDP79T00936A009100230001-1

Declassified in Part - Sanitized Copy Approved for Release 2016/06/14 : CIA-RDP79T00936A009100230001-1

Top Secret

Declassified in Part - Sanitized Copy Approved for Release 2016/06/14 : CIA-RDP79T00936A009100230001-1

Declassified in Part - Sanitized Copy Approved for Release 2016/06/14 : CIA-RDP79T00936A009100240001-0

The President's Daily Brief

27 January 1971

48

Top Secret   50X1

Declassified in Part - Sanitized Copy Approved for Release 2016/06/14 : CIA-RDP79T00936A009100240001-0

Declassified in Part - Sanitized Copy Approved for Release 2016/06/14 : CIA-RDP79T00936A009100240001-0

THE PRESIDENT'S DAILY BRIEF

27 January 1971

PRINCIPAL DEVELOPMENTS   50X1

In Vietnam, the apparent decline in infiltration
continues. *(Page 1)*

(Page 2)

                                                         50X1
                                                         50X1
France. *(Page 3)*

                                                         50X1

Declassified in Part - Sanitized Copy Approved for Release 2016/06/14 : CIA-RDP79T00936A009100240001-0

Declassified in Part - Sanitized Copy Approved for Release 2016/06/14 : CIA-RDP79T00936A009100240001-0

NORTH VIETNAM

Only one infiltration group of about 400 men
has been detected entering the infiltration system
in North Vietnam so far this month. Although
slightly over 2,000 additional troops have been
monitored farther down the system in Laos, these
apparently set out prior to January.

> *The apparent lull in infiltration has now
> entered its fourth week. Since a major
> way station at the northern end of the
> pipeline had previously advised its con-
> tacts that a new group would be setting
> forth nightly between 5 and 10 January.*

50X1

1

Declassified in Part - Sanitized Copy Approved for Release 2016/06/14 : CIA-RDP79T00936A009100240001-0

Declassified in Part - Sanitized Copy Approved for Release 2016/06/14 : CIA-RDP79T00936A009100240001-0

COMMUNIST CHINA - US

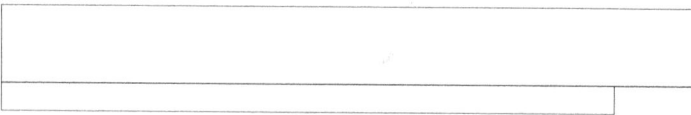

50X1

50X1

Adding to the current chill wind from Peking was the Foreign Ministry statement of Monday that, although breaking no new ground, strongly denounced recent US actions in Indochina. Peking gives no sign of seeing a likelihood of an early resumption of the Warsaw talks. Chinese propaganda, however, continues to avoid bilateral issues dividing Washington and Peking, indicating that China has not closed the door to an eventual resumption of Sino-US contacts.

2

Declassified in Part - Sanitized Copy Approved for Release 2016/06/14 : CIA-RDP79T00936A009100240001-0

Declassified in Part - Sanitized Copy Approved for Release 2016/06/14 : CIA-RDP79T00936A009100240001-0

NOTES

France:    50X1 50X1

                                                  50X1

                                                  50X1

    Uganda: No signs of serious resistance to General Amin's coup have yet developed, and he appears to have a substantial measure of popular support for his ouster of President Obote. None of the other senior army officers has yet been identified as a participant in the coup, however, and some question remains as to Amin's ability to control the army. Obote claimed in a press conference in Dar es Salaam, where he flew from Nairobi yesterday, that he intends to return to Uganda, but he seems unlikely to do so unless Amin's position deteriorates.

3

Declassified in Part - Sanitized Copy Approved for Release 2016/06/14 : CIA-RDP79T00936A009100240001-0

Declassified in Part - Sanitized Copy Approved for Release 2016/06/14 : CIA-RDP79T00936A009100240001-0

Top Secret

Declassified in Part - Sanitized Copy Approved for Release 2016/06/14 : CIA-RDP79T00936A009100240001-0

Declassified in Part - Sanitized Copy Approved for Release 2016/06/14 : CIA-RDP79T00936A009100250001-9

The President's Daily Brief

28 January 1971

46

Top Secret   50X1

Declassified in Part - Sanitized Copy Approved for Release 2016/06/14 : CIA-RDP79T00936A009100250001-9

Declassified in Part - Sanitized Copy Approved for Release 2016/06/14 : CIA-RDP79T00936A009100250001-9

THE PRESIDENT'S DAILY BRIEF

28 January 1971

PRINCIPAL DEVELOPMENTS

The US Embassy in Phnom Penh believes that Communist military strategy still calls for a holding operation in Cambodia. *(Page 1)*

On *Page 2*, we comment on the progress of the Chinese Nationalist irregulars operating against Communist insurgents in northern Thailand.

	Egypt	50X1
		50X1
	(Page 3)	50X1

Armed forces commanders in Argentina are becoming more dissatisfied with President Levingston's policies. *(Page 4)*

Declassified in Part - Sanitized Copy Approved for Release 2016/06/14 : CIA-RDP79T00936A009100250001-9

Declassified in Part - Sanitized Copy Approved for Release 2016/06/14 : CIA-RDP79T00936A009100250001-9

CAMBODIA

A new assessment by the American Embassy of the situation in the wake of the recent enemy harassment of the capital area concludes that Communist strategy still calls for a military holding operation in Cambodia. Enemy action appears to be aimed at pinning down Cambodian Army units and at ensuring the Communists access to bases and sanctuaries essential to their objectives in South Vietnam.

In the embassy's view, as long as the Communists economize in their commitment of main force units in Cambodia, the army will be able to cope with the situation. There is no immediate threat to Phnom Penh that cannot be dealt with by Cambodian forces now in place, together with available air power. The army's morale continues to be good despite recent setbacks, and its capabilities should soon increase with the acquisition of more modern equipment and with the return of battalions now undergoing training in South Vietnam.

The assessment warns that the Cambodian Army's resources, however, are limited. These resources will be under further strain if--as cannot now be ruled out--there is significant development of the military potential of the Khmer Communists who played a part in this week's attacks around Phnom Penh.

The embassy also notes that, while the increased enemy pressure on the capital has caused no break in the essential unity or determination of Cambodia's leaders, it has brought forth new strains and carping among them. There has also been open criticism of the army's effectiveness and this is likely to intensify in the event of further Communist terrorism or successful sapper and mortar attacks against the capital area.

1

Declassified in Part - Sanitized Copy Approved for Release 2016/06/14 : CIA-RDP79T00936A009100250001-9

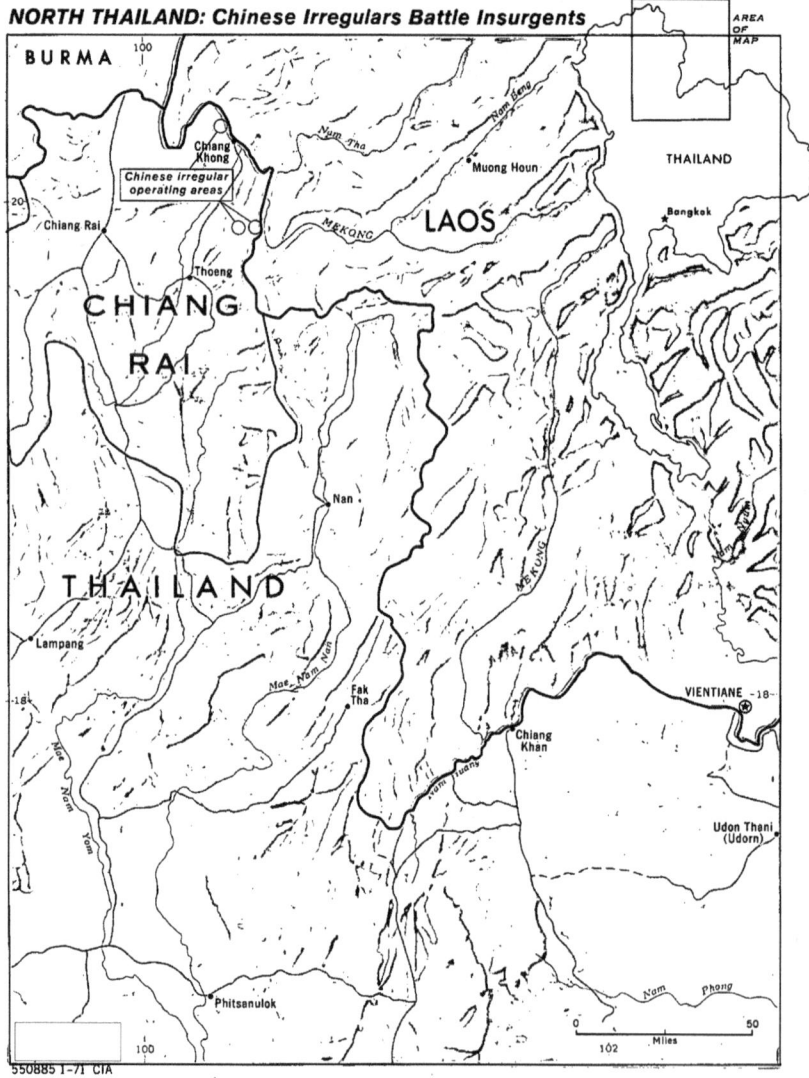

Declassified in Part - Sanitized Copy Approved for Release 2016/06/14 : CIA-RDP79T00936A009100250001-9

NORTH THAILAND: Chinese Irregulars Battle Insurgents

BURMA

Chiang Khong

Chinese irregular operating areas

Chiang Rai

Thoeng

CHIANG RAI

THAILAND

Lampang

Nan

Phitsanulok

Nam Tha

MEKONG

Muong Houn

LAOS

Nam Beng

THAILAND

Bangkok

Mae Nam Nan

Fak Tha

Chiang Khan

MEKONG

VIENTIANE -18-

Udon Thani (Udorn)

Nam Phong

AREA OF MAP

Nam Nom Yom

0   50
0   102   Miles

50X1

550885 1-71 CIA

Declassified in Part - Sanitized Copy Approved for Release 2016/06/14 : CIA-RDP79T00936A009100250001-9

Declassified in Part - Sanitized Copy Approved for Release 2016/06/14 : CIA-RDP79T00936A009100250001-9

THAILAND

The President's Daily Brief of 15 December reported
Bangkok's decision to move some 750 Chinese Nationalist irregulars from the Burmese border to a Communist insurgent area in northern Chiang Rai Province.
Since then, despite stiff resistance, these irregu-
lars--remnants of forces driven from China two dec-
ades ago--have captured two insurgent bases and siz-
able quantities of military equipment and field supplies. The Chinese irregulars were operating under
the direction of the Thai 3rd Army. Bangkok's confidence that the northern insurgency was well in hand
has been shaken by these operations, which have revealed a greater degree of Communist strength in this
region than the Thais anticipated, but there is no
evidence that the Thai Army is willing to join ranks
with the Chinese to drive the insurgents out of
Chiang Rai. Three hundred additional Chinese irregulars are undergoing training and may be available to
reinforce the operation by April.

2

Declassified in Part - Sanitized Copy Approved for Release 2016/06/14 : CIA-RDP79T00936A009100250001-9

Declassified in Part - Sanitized Copy Approved for Release 2016/06/14 : CIA-RDP79T00936A009100250001-9

EGYPT - ARAB STATES

50X1

50X1

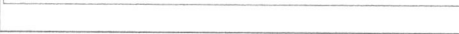

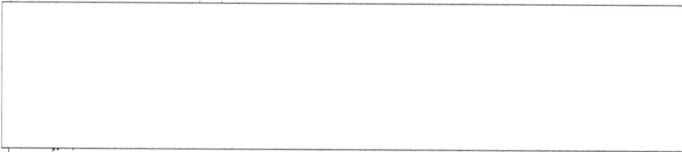

50X1

50X1

50X1

50X1

50X1

50X1

50X1

3

Declassified in Part - Sanitized Copy Approved for Release 2016/06/14 : CIA-RDP79T00936A009100250001-9

Declassified in Part - Sanitized Copy Approved for Release 2016/06/14 : CIA-RDP79T00936A009100250001-9

NOTE

Argentina: [   ] army
commander in chief General Lanusse and the air force
and navy commanders are grumbling about the policies
of President Levingston, and hope to meet with him
early next week to air their complaints. The major
source of their disenchantment lies in the manner
and timing of the planned return to "constitutional
processes." Levingston plans to hold elections in
four to five years, but Lanusse believes they should
be held sooner and that they must be carefully controlled to prevent victory by a leftist coalition.
Lanusse admits that Levingston's removal would cause
grave damage to Argentina but maintains that the
service commanders are prepared to take this risk if
the President does not accept their recommendations.

50X1

4

Declassified in Part - Sanitized Copy Approved for Release 2016/06/14 : CIA-RDP79T00936A009100250001-9

Declassified in Part - Sanitized Copy Approved for Release 2016/06/14 : CIA-RDP79T00936A009100250001-9

Top Secret

Declassified in Part - Sanitized Copy Approved for Release 2016/06/14 : CIA-RDP79T00936A009100250001-9

Declassified in Part - Sanitized Copy Approved for Release 2016/06/14 : CIA-RDP79T00936A009100260001-8

The President's Daily Brief

29 January 1971

Top Secret 50X1

Declassified in Part - Sanitized Copy Approved for Release 2016/06/14 : CIA-RDP79T00936A009100260001-8

Declassified in Part - Sanitized Copy Approved for Release 2016/06/14 : CIA-RDP79T00936A009100260001-8

THE PRESIDENT'S DAILY BRIEF

29 January 1971

PRINCIPAL DEVELOPMENTS

In Laos, the Communists are increasing their troop strength west of the Plaine des Jarres prior to the dry season campaign. *(Page 1)*

Government clearing operations around Phnom Penh proceeded smoothly yesterday. *(Page 2)*

50X1

(Page 3) 50X1

Some comments on the Israeli reply to Jarring appear on *Page 4*.

50X1

A progress report on Chinese road building in Laos appears on *Page 6*.

Declassified in Part - Sanitized Copy Approved for Release 2016/06/14 : CIA-RDP79T00936A009100260001-8

Declassified in Part - Sanitized Copy Approved for Release 2016/06/14 : CIA-RDP79T00936A009100260001-8

LAOS/PLAINE DES JARRES: Buildup of NVA Forces

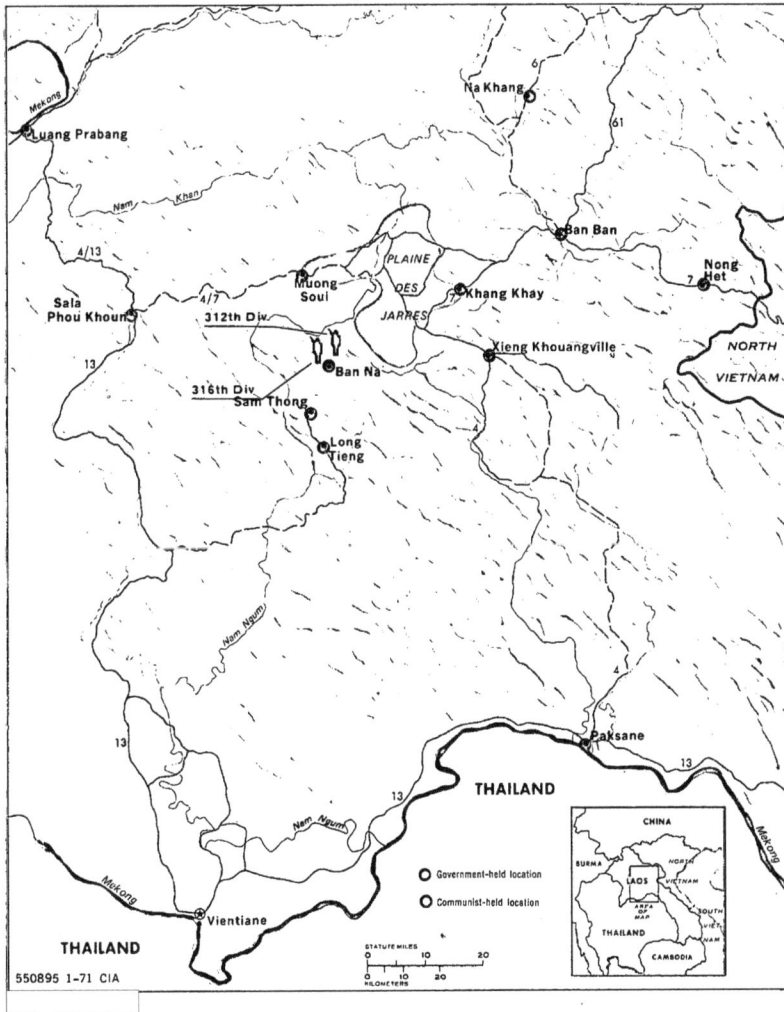

Na Khang

Luang Prabang

Nam Khan

4/13

4/7

Muong Soui

PLAINE DES JARRES

Ban Ban

Nong Het

Khang Khay

Sala Phou Khoun

312th Div

Ban Na

Xieng Khouangville

NORTH VIETNAM

316th Div

Sam Thong

Long Tieng

13

13

Nam Ngum

Paksane

13

13

THAILAND

Nam Ngum

○ Government-held location
○ Communist-held location

CHINA

BURMA

LAOS

NORTH VIETNAM

THAILAND

AREA OF MAP

SOUTH VIET NAM

CAMBODIA

Mekong

THAILAND

Vientiane

Mekong

550895 1-71 CIA

STATUTE MILES
0   10   20

KILOMETERS
0   10   20

50X1

Declassified in Part - Sanitized Copy Approved for Release 2016/06/14 : CIA-RDP79T00936A009100260001-8

Declassified in Part - Sanitized Copy Approved for Release 2016/06/14 : CIA-RDP79T00936A009100260001-8

LAOS

Major portions of the North Vietnamese 316th Division have moved near Ban Na, which commands the northern approaches to the main government irregular base at Long Tieng. Two elements of the 312th NVA Division are also in the region, and other parts of the 312th Division continue to move into northern Laos from North Vietnam.

> *The Communists now have more than 2,000 troops around Ban Na. Units of the 316th are continuing to engage in tactical operations and reconnaissance around Ban Na, Sam Thong, and Long Tieng, indicating that they may remain in the area along with newly arrived elements of the 312th.*

> *Although their precise targets and timing are not clear, the extent of the enemy buildup suggests that the Communists plan to begin their drive within the next few weeks, earlier than last year's effort which began in late February.*

1

Declassified in Part - Sanitized Copy Approved for Release 2016/06/14 : CIA-RDP79T00936A009100260001-8

Declassified in Part - Sanitized Copy Approved for Release 2016/06/14 : CIA-RDP79T00936A009100260001-8

CAMBODIA

Cambodian forces are encountering little enemy resistance as they continue clearing operations around Phnom Penh. An intercepted Cambodian Army message claims that several large enemy columns equipped with heavy weapons were converging yesterday on Phnom Penh from the Kompong Cham area. Another said that Communist troops were setting up rocket launching sites in several villages west of the Phnom Penh airfield.

> *The details of these reports are pretty clearly exaggerated, but the enemy is capable of carrying out new attacks near the capital. Intercepts show that the headquarters of the North Vietnamese 96th Artillery Regiment was 15 miles northeast of Phnom Penh yesterday, about seven miles closer than its previous location. An enemy artillery element--possibly from the 96th--has been detected 20 miles east of the capital, in good position to threaten traffic on the Mekong.*

2

Declassified in Part - Sanitized Copy Approved for Release 2016/06/14 : CIA-RDP79T00936A009100260001-8

Declassified in Part - Sanitized Copy Approved for Release 2016/06/14 : CIA-RDP79T00936A009100260001-8

USSR–UAR

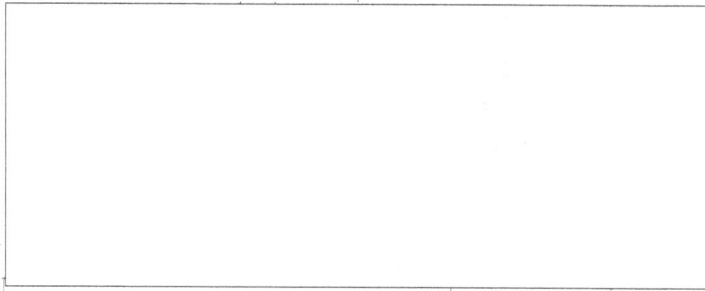

50X1

50X1

50X1

50X1

3

Declassified in Part - Sanitized Copy Approved for Release 2016/06/14 : CIA-RDP79T00936A009100260001-8

Declassified in Part - Sanitized Copy Approved for Release 2016/06/14 : CIA-RDP79T00936A009100260001-8

MIDDLE EAST

The text of the Israeli reply passed to Jarring on 27 January does not appear to provide Jarring with any additional aid in persuading the Egyptians to agree to an extension of the cease-fire. The Israelis criticize the Egyptian note of 18 January as failing to take note of many points covered in the 9 January Israeli "Essentials of Peace" proposals.

The latest Israeli paper does not address itself directly to the question of Israeli withdrawal from the occupied territories or the refugee question. First, say the Israelis, specific agreement must be reached on four points:

--peace in the area;

--respect for and acknowledgment of the sovereignty, territorial integrity and political independence of every state in the area;

--mutual acknowledgment of the rights of each other to live in peace within secure and recognized boundaries free from threats or acts of force; and

--termination of all claims of belligerency by each state against the other.

Once this is accomplished, the Israeli reply states, then it will be possible to discuss other issues.

4

Declassified in Part - Sanitized Copy Approved for Release 2016/06/14 : CIA-RDP79T00936A009100260001-8

Declassified in Part - Sanitized Copy Approved for Release 2016/06/14 : CIA-RDP79T00936A009100260001-8

50X1

5

Declassified in Part - Sanitized Copy Approved for Release 2016/06/14 : CIA-RDP79T00936A009100260001-8

Declassified in Part - Sanitized Copy Approved for Release 2016/06/14 : CIA-RDP79T00936A009100260001-8

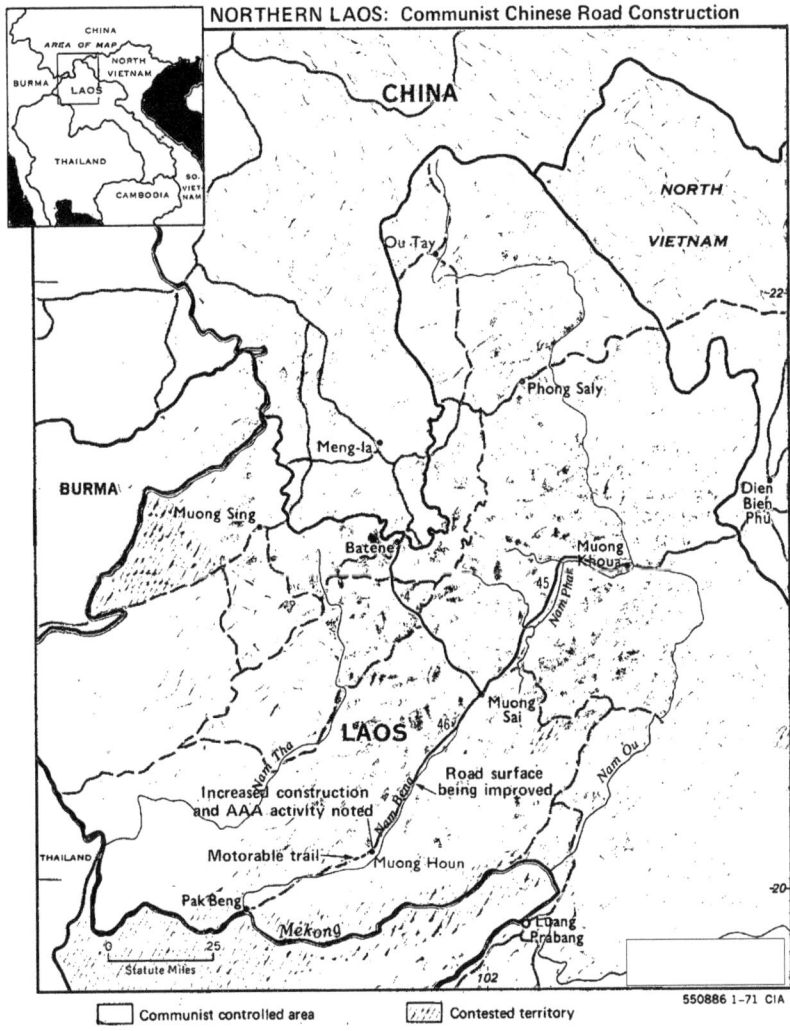

NORTHERN LAOS: Communist Chinese Road Construction

Communist controlled area   Contested territory

550886 1–71 CIA

50X1

Declassified in Part - Sanitized Copy Approved for Release 2016/06/14 : CIA-RDP79T00936A009100260001-8

Declassified in Part - Sanitized Copy Approved for Release 2016/06/14 : CIA-RDP79T00936A009100260001-8

NOTE

Communist China - Laos: The Chinese appear to be preparing to resume construction of Route 46 toward the Mekong. Photography of early January shows increased activity just north of Muong Houn, the present terminus of the road, including the expansion of construction camps and the building of new AAA sites. So far this dry season Chinese road builders have concentrated on finishing Route 45, which runs northeast from Muong Sai to Muong Khoua, and on improving the surface of Route 46 between Muong Sai and Muong Houn. Both projects are nearly completed.

6

Declassified in Part - Sanitized Copy Approved for Release 2016/06/14 : CIA-RDP79T00936A009100260001-8

Declassified in Part - Sanitized Copy Approved for Release 2016/06/14 : CIA-RDP79T00936A009100260001-8

Top Secret

Declassified in Part - Sanitized Copy Approved for Release 2016/06/14 : CIA-RDP79T00936A009100260001-8

Declassified in Part - Sanitized Copy Approved for Release 2016/06/14 : CIA-RDP79T00936A009100270001-7

The President's Daily Brief

30 January 1971

48

~~Top Secret~~ 50X1

Declassified in Part - Sanitized Copy Approved for Release 2016/06/14 : CIA-RDP79T00936A009100270001-7

Declassified in Part - Sanitized Copy Approved for Release 2016/06/14 : CIA-RDP79T00936A009100270001-7

THE PRESIDENT'S DAILY BRIEF

30 January 1971

PRINCIPAL DEVELOPMENTS

Thai Foreign Minister Thanat has taken a hard line toward Washington in recent conversations with Commonwealth diplomats in Bangkok. *(Page 1)*

The international oil negotiations are discussed on *Page 3.*

Egypt is taking steps to increase its military preparedness as the end of the formal cease-fire period nears. *(Page 4)*

The Panamanians have outlined their objectives in forthcoming Canal treaty negotiations. *(Page 5)*

50X1

Argentina

(Page 6)

50X1
50X1

Declassified in Part - Sanitized Copy Approved for Release 2016/06/14 : CIA-RDP79T00936A009100270001-7

Declassified in Part - Sanitized Copy Approved for Release 2016/06/14 : CIA-RDP79T00936A009100270001-7

THAILAND

Foreign Minister Thanat took a very hard line toward Washington in several recent conversations with members of the Commonwealth's diplomatic corps in Thailand.

The British ambassador to Thailand told Ambassador Unger yesterday that he had participated in three significant parleys with Thanat, apparently at the latter's initiative, within the past two weeks. In these Thanat railed against US policy in Indochina, arguing that the French were the only ones working for a negotiated settlement of the war. He said that he favored Big Minh over Thieu and Ky in the coming presidential race in South Vietnam because Minh could negotiate successfully with the Communists.

In one of the conversations on 26 January which included the British, Canadian and Indian ambassadors, Thanat claimed he had received a clear message from Hanoi that they were looking for someone who could get the Paris negotiations off dead center and facilitate a peaceful settlement in Southeast Asia.

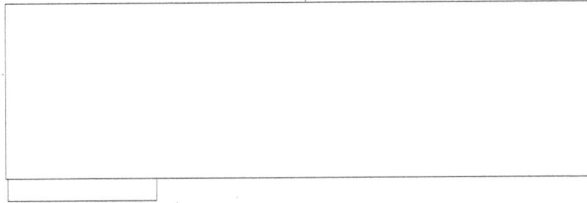

50X1

50X1

Thanat said that while the North Vietnamese may have had him in mind as their peacebroker, Thailand was in no position to play such a role, but the Canadians were. He said that he would propose to Hanoi that they get in touch with Canadian Ambassador Cox on this score.

In discussing a peace settlement, Thanat stated that he was prepared to accept Communist domination of South Vietnam, Cambodia, and Laos. Thailand, he said, would be able to hold its own and not fall into the Communist camp. In making these statements, Thanat gave no indication that they had the blessing of other Thai leaders, although he said a day-long cabinet meeting had preceded his remarks.

(continued)

1

Declassified in Part - Sanitized Copy Approved for Release 2016/06/14 : CIA-RDP79T00936A009100270001-7

Declassified in Part - Sanitized Copy Approved for Release 2016/06/14 : CIA-RDP79T00936A009100270001-7

For over two years Thanat has been in the forefront of those Thai leaders who have been pressing for a more flexible and independent foreign policy--in short, a policy calling for improved relations with Communist countries as a hedge against the diminishing US presence in Southeast Asia. In addition to his flirtations with Peking, Moscow, and Hanoi, Thanat has led the recent criticism against Washington's proposed sale of PL-480 rice and surplus rubber to some of Thailand's traditional Asian markets.

Although Thanat has in the past exercised considerable influence over Thailand's foreign policy, he has made relatively little headway recently in redirecting its course. His failure is in part the consequence of recent events in Cambodia and Laos which have increased Thailand's dependence on the US for its security. Thailand's room for diplomatic maneuver has been further circumscribed by Peking's failure to pick up public and private overtures from Bangkok.

There is also a continuing question of how much support Thanat can command from Bangkok's military leadership for important shifts in the country's foreign policy. In particular, it is unclear where Prime Minister Thanom's heir-apparent, General Praphat--a staunch anti-Communist and strong advocate of close US ties--stands. Praphat's relations with Thanat have been strained for some time.

2

Declassified in Part - Sanitized Copy Approved for Release 2016/06/14 : CIA-RDP79T00936A009100270001-7

Declassified in Part - Sanitized Copy Approved for Release 2016/06/14 : CIA-RDP79T00936A009100270001-7

INTERNATIONAL OIL

Oil company representatives and the Persian Gulf committee of the Organization of Petroleum Exporting Countries (OPEC) exchanged substantive proposals Thursday, the first such exchange since the discussions began on 19 January. As expected, the offers are far apart--for example, OPEC countries have demanded a posted price increase of 54 cents per barrel, while the companies are offering 15 cents.

The head of the oil company team has told the American Embassy in Tehran that he is disturbed at the wide disparity between the offers and believes a settlement close to what oil companies see as reasonable will be difficult to achieve. The general consensus of industry negotiators is that the situation is "gloomy but not hopeless." Iranian negotiators are talking optimistically about an early settlement, but this is in part to avoid drastic action, such as production cutbacks or shutdowns that radical producing countries may urge when all OPEC countries meet in Tehran on 3 February.

Libya still refuses to meet with oil company representatives in the parallel negotiations that the companies are trying to start in Tripoli. The Libyans insist on separate talks with each company. Libyan officials have refused to receive the oil companies' joint proposal--the equivalent of the one presented Thursday to the Persian Gulf group--although they say it can be mailed to them. The Libyans appear uncertain at this point as to their next step. Oil Minister Mabruk has threatened, however, that "a dangerous situation" will exist on 3 February if the oil companies have not reached separate settlements with the Libyan Government by that time.

Syria's agreement to reopen the damaged Trans-Arabian pipeline, out of service since last May, could reduce slightly Libya's leverage in the negotiations. TAPLINE officials estimate that 500,000 barrels per day of Saudi Arabian oil will reach Mediterranean ports by the end of next week. This is 15 percent of current production in Libya. In addition, the availability in the Mediterranean of another 500,000 barrels per day of "short-haul" oil for Europe will ease the tight world tanker situation by increasing transport capability by about three percent.

3

Declassified in Part - Sanitized Copy Approved for Release 2016/06/14 : CIA-RDP79T00936A009100270001-7

Declassified in Part - Sanitized Copy Approved for Release 2016/06/14 : CIA-RDP79T00936A009100270001-7

EGYPT-ISRAEL

[_____] press reports that Egypt is taking steps to increase its military preparedness as the end of the formal cease-fire period nears.

50X1

50X1

All this has been accompanied by a chorus from Egypt's public media about the failure of various efforts to achieve any diplomatic progress and the inability of Cairo to extend the cease-fire without tangible results in the political sphere.

Egyptian leaders evidently hope that the creation of a warlike atmosphere will increase pressure on Israel to make a substantive offer on the issue of withdrawal. Some of Cairo's actions, however, are only normal defensive precautions taken in light of the uncertainty that will prevail if the cease-fire is not formally renewed. Although Egypt no doubt has various contingency plans for military actions against Israeli forces in the Sinai, there are no indications now that any such operation is imminent. Israel likewise has displayed no intentions to resume hostilities but as usual is on the alert for any contingency.

4

Declassified in Part - Sanitized Copy Approved for Release 2016/06/14 : CIA-RDP79T00936A009100270001-7

Declassified in Part - Sanitized Copy Approved for Release 2016/06/14 : CIA-RDP79T00936A009100270001-7

PANAMA

> *A six-point Panamanian position paper in-*
> *dicates that Panama will stress questions*
> *of sovereignty, territorial jurisdiction,*
> *and economic benefits in forthcoming Canal*
> *treaty negotiations.*

According to the paper, Panama will demand full
political, fiscal, labor, judicial and administrative
jurisdiction over the Canal Zone. Panama acknowl-
edges a need for US technical and administrative know-
how, but calls for increasing Panamanian participation in the operation and maintenance of the Canal
and for greatly expanded commercial and economic
concessions. Panama wants the US military presence
to be limited to Canal defense and to be "for a limited period of time with the cooperation of the Panamanian armed forces."

Foreign Minister Tack told Deputy Assistant Secretary of State Hurwitch on Thursday that while Panama would not accept a perpetuity clause, it would
not insist on a fixed termination date for defense
arrangements and would accept a Canal treaty that
could be revised every 20-25 years to meet changing
conditions. Tack said that any transfer of jurisdiction over the Zone could be programmed over a number of years.

> *This initial presentation has come more*
> *than a year after General Torrijos first*
> *expressed an interest in resuming negotia-*
> *tions, but the Panamanians are likely to*
> *push now for a more rapid negotiating pace.*
> *The government's urgency will increase sub-*
> *stantially by summer as its budget prob-*
> *lems mount. As negotiations proceed, there*
> *will be always the danger that the erratic*
> *Torrijos will react impulsively to any de-*
> *lays or setbacks.*

Declassified in Part - Sanitized Copy Approved for Release 2016/06/14 : CIA-RDP79T00936A009100270001-7

Declassified in Part - Sanitized Copy Approved for Release 2016/06/14 : CIA-RDP79T00936A009100270001-7

SUDAN: Israelis Aiding Rebels in Mining the Nile River

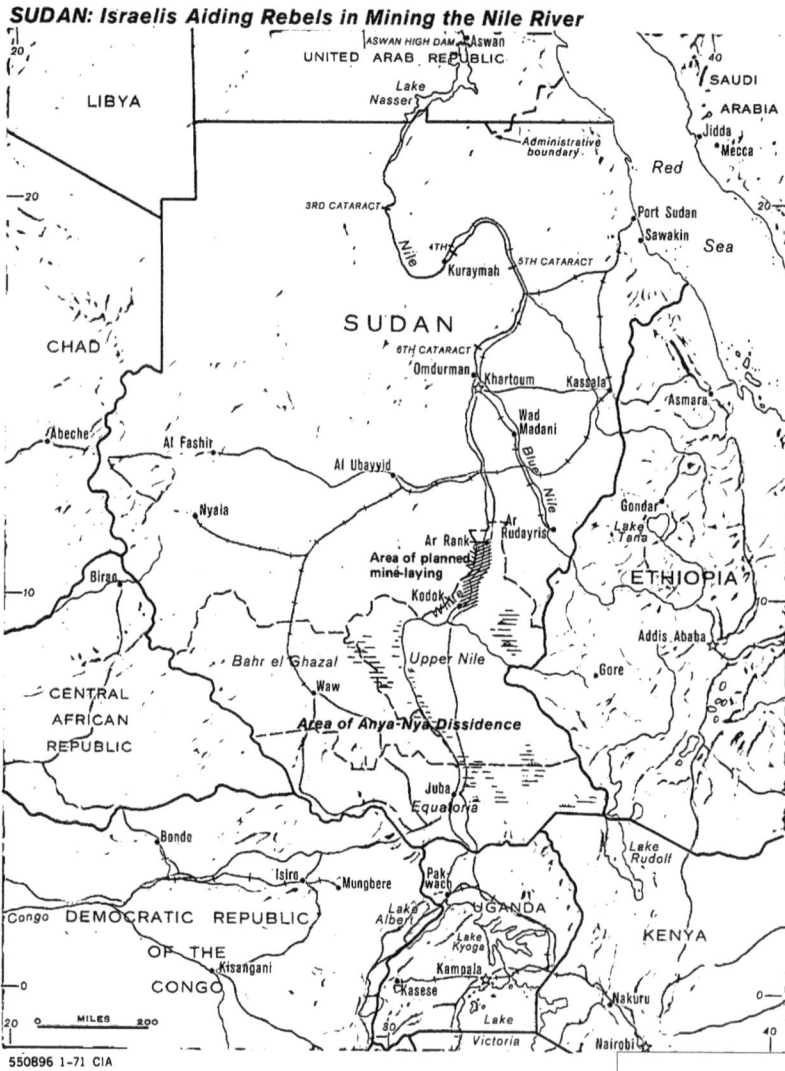

550896 1-71 CIA

50X1

Declassified in Part - Sanitized Copy Approved for Release 2016/06/14 : CIA-RDP79T00936A009100270001-7

FOR THE PRESIDENT ONLY

NOTES

50X1

50X1
50X1
50X1

Argentina:

50X1

Laos: Government harassing operations against the Communist infiltration corridor in the central panhandle (south of Muong Nong where the Communists have built a new road) are continuing to meet only moderate resistance. There are indications, however, that stiffer opposition may be in the offing, possibly involving a regiment of the North Vietnamese 320th Division that recently entered Laos and may be on the move in this general area.

6

Declassified in Part - Sanitized Copy Approved for Release 2016/06/14 : CIA-RDP79T00936A009100270001-7

Top Secret

Declassified in Part - Sanitized Copy Approved for Release 2016/06/14 : CIA-RDP79T00936A009100270001-7

Declassified in Part - Sanitized Copy Approved for Release 2016/06/14 : CIA-RDP79T00936A009100280001-6

The President's Daily Brief

31 *Sunday Cable*
January 1971

13

50X1

Top Secret

Declassified in Part - Sanitized Copy Approved for Release 2016/06/14 : CIA-RDP79T00936A009100280001-6

Declassified in Part - Sanitized Copy Approved for Release 2016/06/14 : CIA-RDP79T00936A009100280001-6

CAMBODIA

The first convoy of petroleum for Phnom Penh from the
refinery at Kompong Som was ambushed, despite air cover,
on 30 January by Communist troops along Route 4 about 42
miles north of Kompong Som. Preliminary reports indicate
that several of the 31 tanker trucks were set afire and that
the remainder headed back to Kompong Som. There have been
several enemy harassing attacks against government positions in the same general area in the past few days.

Route 4, closed since November, had been declared
officially open to civilian traffic during daylight hours
by the local Cambodian commander, Sosthene Fernandez.

50X1

that his forces could keep the road clear between Veal
Renh and the Pich Nil pass, the stretch where the ambush
later occurred, although his units farther north near the
pass were being harassed.

A riverine POL convoy from South Vietnam arrived safely
in Phnom Penh on 29 January. It is the first such resupply
mission to reach the capital since 17 January. The convoy,
consisting of four oil barges and three tugs carrying
1,226,700 gallons of petroleum supplies, encountered two
minor enemy harassments during the trip, but sustained no
damage.

Declassified in Part - Sanitized Copy Approved for Release 2016/06/14 : CIA-RDP79T00936A009100280001-6

Declassified in Part - Sanitized Copy Approved for Release 2016/06/14 : CIA-RDP79T00936A009100280001-6

NOTES

Laos:  50X1

Declassified in Part - Sanitized Copy Approved for Release 2016/06/14 : CIA-RDP79T00936A009100280001-6

Declassified in Part - Sanitized Copy Approved for Release 2016/06/14 : CIA-RDP79T00936A009100280001-6

Top Secret

Declassified in Part - Sanitized Copy Approved for Release 2016/06/14 : CIA-RDP79T00936A009100280001-6

www.ingramcontent.com/pod-product-compliance
Lightning Source LLC
Chambersburg PA
CBHW061834260326
41914CB00005B/999